FROM ZERO TO
MILLIONAIRE

Every owner of a physical copy of this edition of

FROM ZERO TO MILLIONAIRE

can download the eBook for free direct from us at Harriman House, in a DRM-free format that can be read on any eReader, tablet or smartphone.

Simply head to:

ebooks.harriman-house.com/ fromzerotomillionaire

to get your copy now.

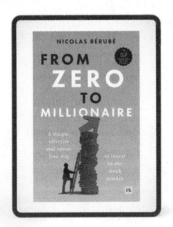

FROM ZERO TO MILLIONAIRE

A simple, effective, and stress-free
way to invest in the stock market

NICOLAS BÉRUBÉ

HARRIMAN HOUSE LTD
3 Viceroy Court
Bedford Road
Petersfield
Hampshire
GU32 3LJ
GREAT BRITAIN
Tel: +44 (0)1730 233870

Email: enquiries@harriman-house.com
Website: harriman.house

First published in English in 2023.

Originally published in Canada in 2022 as *De Zéro À Millionnaire*.

Copyright © Nicolas Bérubé

The right of Nicolas Bérubé to be identified as the Author has been asserted in accordance with the Copyright, Design and Patents Act 1988.

Paperback ISBN: 978-1-80409-026-8
eBook ISBN: 978-1-80409-027-5

British Library Cataloguing in Publication Data
A CIP catalogue record for this book can be obtained from the British Library.

To Pénélope, who enlightens me

CONTENTS

PREFACE

"You don't seem to give much thought to the matter in hand," I said at last, interrupting Holmes.

"No data yet," he answered. "It is a capital mistake to theorize before you have all the evidence. It biases the judgement."

Arthur Conan Doyle, The Adventures of Sherlock Holmes

I'm not an investor. People always tell me, you should have your money working for you. I've decided I'll do the work. I'm gonna let the money relax.

Jerry Seinfeld, comedian

THE PILE OF books cluttering my bedside table threatened to collapse on my head overnight, but my mind was elsewhere – I was about to get rich.

I was 33 years old and living in the Silver Lake area of Los Angeles, a bohemian-chic neighborhood of the West Coast megalopolis. I was convinced that the stock market was about to crash.

The year was 2010 and the U.S. economy was in free fall. We were experiencing the greatest financial crisis since the Great Depression of the 1930s. On Wall Street, hundreds of employees of major banks and investment firms had recently emerged from their office towers, staring blankly, cardboard boxes under their arms. In my neighborhood, dozens of empty commercial spaces were for sale or rent. The decline of America was palpable. It seemed endless.

After falling violently, the U.S. stock market had rebounded by a whopping 60% in just a few months. Many observers believed that this rally was meaningless, that a new and deeper correction was imminent. I was one of them.

I had just finished reading several books about the financial crisis, including *The Big Short*,[1] by Michael Lewis, and *The Greatest Trade Ever*,[2] by Gregory Zuckerman, which told the story of how astute investors predicted the bursting of the U.S. housing bubble and positioned themselves to profit. I was fascinated by the story of these stubborn people who endured the ridicule of their peers in the good years and then became wise visionaries when the market crashed.

This time, I decided, the visionary would be me.

I had just made a $10,000 profit on the resale of an apartment in Montreal. I decided to invest this amount in a simple idea: that Wall Street would collapse.

To place my bet, I bought put options, which are financial products that increase in value if the price of the stock to which they are linked falls. I had to open a brokerage account that allowed me to trade on the Chicago Stock Exchange.

I had never done this before: I learned what to do by reading authors and bloggers who thought, like I did, that the market was going to crash. My plan was to add money to my bet as soon as the market tipped in my favor. I put in the energy and determination of someone who sees what few others are willing to consider.

From day one, I lost money.

Every time I checked my brokerage account, my heart stopped beating: my $10,000 had melted away by a few hundred dollars. Not only was the stock market refusing to collapse, it was still going up!

I wasn't going to be discouraged. You can't climb a mountain without getting scratched.

After a few months, the result was clear: I had failed. My options were worth a few hundred dollars when I resigned myself to selling them. If investing in the stock market was an exam, I had received my corrected paper, marked with a big "zero" written in red ink.

I don't know if $10,000 is a lot of money to you or not. I remember that losing that amount so quickly was unpleasant enough to make me think about it often.

I still can't explain it to myself, but rather than banish them from my life, I decided to figure out how the financial markets worked.

In the years that followed, I spent thousands of hours reading about finance and investing. I was able to interview some of the most prolific investors and financial writers of our time, including Mohnish Pabrai, Morgan Housel, Andrew Hallam, Peter Adeney (the wildly popular blogger who writes under the pen name of Mr. Money Mustache), and many others. I absorbed the history of the markets, and learned about the mistakes made by most investors and the proven ways to make long-term investments. I took an in-depth look at the lives and writings of financial giants, including Warren Buffett, Charlie Munger, Benjamin Graham, and John Bogle, who are considered some of the greatest investors in history. Like kids in a candy store, Buffett and Munger were buying stocks with their hands full while I was busy betting on the stock market apocalypse...

I realized that in my rush to get rich, I had broken all the rules that have governed successful stock market investing for over 400 years.

I realized that the stock market is not a casino, nor is it a game of daring or trickery. That for generations, those who thought they could make a quick buck have found themselves in my situation – with a bloody lip.

I also saw that this world I had imagined to be barren was populated by fascinating characters, fortunes won and lost, and the full range of human emotions, multiplied tenfold by the prospect of financial gain, one of the most powerful intoxicants that ever existed.

Two years after my embarrassing failure, I started investing again. This time, I didn't regret it.

I have since learned that all investors have made mistakes. Even Warren Buffett says he lost 20% of his money on an unfortunate investment he made in his early 20s, when he didn't have the experience to understand what he was doing.

That 20% that went up in smoke would be worth billions of dollars today. "Fairly big mistake," he once quipped.[3]

The purpose of this book is to prevent you from seeing thousands of dollars disappear before you become a good investor. (If you already have, I'm sorry! Some lessons hurt more than others.)

LEARNING THE LESSONS

The thrust of my first book published in French, *Les Millionnaires ne sont pas ceux que vous croyez* (*Millionaires Are Not Who You Think They Are*), was that wealth is not found in the hope of a pay raise or a big year-end bonus, nor is it found in the pursuit of an exceptional investment. Wealth is found in the choices we make with the money we have now, today.

I gave a series of lectures after the publication of the book. At the end of each presentation, I took 30 or 40 minutes to talk with the people who came to hear me.

I expected to have to answer questions about the lives of the millionaires I interviewed or to justify the statistics I was putting forward. I received no such questions.

What everyone who raised their hand wanted to know was how to invest in the stock market.

When I returned home after these conferences, I was happy to have had these exchanges. At the same time, I felt a little dizzy. Partly because of me, people might become investors.

It's almost as if, by talking about a beautiful faraway land, I convinced them to grab a backpack, some hiking boots, and get going. I knew they were making the right decision. I also knew that there would be difficulties, doubts, and fears along the way: I lived it, and I continue to live it every day.

These are the thoughts that led me to write this book.

As I talk about investing, I notice that the subject is full of myths, preconceived notions, and disturbing beliefs: money has always been a magnet for questionable strategies.

At a time when more people in the Western world are investing in the stock market than ever before, I realize that many investors feel that they are missing out on something. We hear our friends and colleagues talk about how well they are doing, and we wonder why our own investments seem to be stalling. Should we buy stocks in more exciting companies? Change financial planners or portfolio managers? Find someone special, someone who can find stocks that will increase in value dramatically over time? This book will attempt to answer these questions.

Investing is a simple activity, which a whole industry strives to make complicated to justify its existence. So let me cover some important lessons in these pages so that you don't make the mistakes I did to acquire them.

Nicolas Bérubé

INTRODUCTION: "IT'S ALL GOING TO COLLAPSE"

If you're not sure what to be alarmed about, everything is alarming.

Chris Hadfield, Canadian astronaut

"I DON'T THINK THE United States is going to survive."

Several years ago, I was having lunch with a friend in a San Francisco restaurant when he made this confession.

Around us, young waiters brought fair trade espressos and gluten-free bread to customers dressed in relaxed yet sophisticated attire. Near the entrance, yoga mats rolled up in specialized covers lay jumbled together like multicolored offerings to the gods of wellness and self-discovery.

I had just said that I was optimistic about the future of the United States. My friend, apparently, was not.

"The only thing keeping Wall Street alive is the devaluation of the dollar," he said. "The dollar is no longer backed by gold. The U.S. economy will collapse. There's no escaping it."

"It's been a long time since gold was used as collateral for the U.S. currency," I replied.

"Yes, but little by little people are realizing that."

I asked my friend if he was the type to have canned goods in his basement to be ready in case of disaster.

"We have enough food to last a year," he said.

I took a bite of hash browns. Behind him, a lady was parking a BMW station wagon along the sidewalk.

"Yep, I'm a *prepper*," he added with a smile, able to laugh at himself.

"Do you buy gold?" I asked.

"Of course! But you have to buy physical gold, otherwise it's worthless. I'm in the process of arranging to have the gold stored. By the way, why do you think the Americans are in Afghanistan? It's for the rare-earth elements! Same thing with Mali... A few families control the world banking system... They support Wall Street... It's all going to collapse."

A decade has passed since the morning of our conversation. In that time, U.S. stock markets – which account for more than half of the total value of all stock markets around the world – have quadrupled in value, advancing almost relentlessly in line with corporate productivity and profits.

The price of gold is lower than the day when we had our lunch.

My friend was a brilliant guy who worked in the demanding world of San Francisco technology companies. He was a professional who lived in a nice house in one of the nicest neighborhoods in one of the most admired cities on Earth.

I am not telling this story to show that my friend was wrong. As I wrote in the Preface, I myself foresaw a dramatic stock market crash, which came very close to ending my fledgling investment career.

I tell it because if you talk to people about stock market investments, you're likely to quickly hear fearmongering: "It's a casino!" Or, "It's all going to crash, wake up!"

A few years ago, during a Christmas party, a family member told me that a stock market apocalypse was about to happen.

"I sold everything," he told me, a bottle of beer in hand, the Christmas tree glittering behind him. "The stock market has gone up a lot and is breaking record after record. I have a bad feeling... I think the next crash will be as devastating as ever."

A few months later, one of my neighbors mentioned the same fear. "We're due for a good drubbing," he revealed.

As it turned out, they weren't completely wrong: the market did eventually experience downturns in the years that followed. But the market is now higher than when they made these dark predictions.

My sampling is small and anecdotal, I admit. But around me, it is almost always men who believe they know how to listen to their *gut* to know the future of the markets. And, like the examples cited here, they are mostly highly educated men who are competent in their field and have enviable careers.

This hunch that imminent chaos is about to strike can seduce the bravest person, and the most experienced market expert.

This hunch is worthless. I will explain why.

THE SUPERPOWERS OF INVESTORS

Investing is a strange practice, which has its origin in a renunciation. To invest is to give up spending money now to have more money later.

Why do it?

In fact, the question should be: do we have a choice?

Our government pensions and annuities were designed to supplement retirement income – not replace it. The number of employers offering attractive retirement plans is falling. And if you're self-employed or an entrepreneur, you don't need me to tell you that you must fund your own lifestyle, which will likely last for decades after you stop working.

Investing has risks. *Not* investing carries far greater risks.

Rather than treading water from paycheck to paycheck, buying financial assets allows us to gain freedom – and enjoy it – throughout our lives.

Taking a year off to travel, not needing the bank to buy a car or property, dealing with a costly contingency in seconds, or making generous donations to those in need, are just some of the superpowers that investors possess.

Because investing is not taught in school, many people believe that it is too complicated, too risky, or too abstract, without realizing that investing well is extremely simple, and within virtually everyone's reach.

As a result, many people buy a house or apartment and pay the mortgage without seeing the value of investing elsewhere – they don't realize that they are missing out on an opportunity for wealth that is light years away from the gains that residential real estate can make.

If the gains from the sale of a home are striking, it is because, for most of us, it is the only time in our lives that we are faced with amounts in the hundreds of thousands of dollars or more. Without a point of comparison, the price of a home, even a modest one, takes on an impressive value that never ceases to fascinate.

Investor Warren Buffett bought his current home in Omaha, Nebraska, in 1958. He paid $31,500 for it. His property is now valued at $700,000. But if he had invested his $31,500 in the stock market instead, that investment would be worth over $23 million today.

Is it any wonder that Buffett has spent his life buying businesses and not villas, and that he has referred to his house as "Buffett's folly"?

The reason the rich are getting richer faster than the rest of the population is that they are not letting most of their net worth sleep in the walls that protect them from the rain and wind. The rich get richer because they buy financial assets, such as stocks (also called equities), mutual funds, and bonds.

40%

The top 1% of the wealthiest Americans have 40% of their net worth invested in stocks and mutual funds, while the bottom 50% in terms of wealth on average only hold 2% of their assets in these types of investments.

For a long time, only the wealthy had the means and contacts to invest in these other types of assets. This is no longer true. Of course, having little money is a hindrance to investing, but not an insurmountable obstacle. Starting to invest $5 a day at the age of 20 can make us millionaires in retirement. Without taking unnecessary risks. Without reading financial newspapers or becoming a finance nerd.

You don't need to have worn out the benches of business schools to become a great investor. In fact, the further you are from business schools, the more of an innate advantage you have in growing your money. That's what you'll discover in this book.

Books that teach investing in the stock market often assume that with the necessary tools to distinguish promising companies, investors can go ahead and build a portfolio that will grow nicely over the years.

Yet researchers have shown that our emotions and behavior contribute far more to our success than the value of any publicly traded company.

The latest studies also show that spending our energy and time looking for stocks that will make us richer essentially makes us poorer.

Indeed, you will discover that it is more advantageous to buy the whole haystack than to spend your time looking for the needle. This is a counterintuitive strategy, but one that will pay off and allow you to join the leading group of the best investors on the planet. You'll beat the returns of financial professionals – those highly paid, educated people who drive around in luxury vehicles to manage millions of dollars from their downtown towers.

Through these pages, I will show you how to get better returns than the pros and experience fewer declines in market storms. All this, while spending less than one hour per year managing your investments.

And if you choose to have a professional handle your investments, you'll learn how to select someone who will charge transparent and reasonable fees, and who will work in your best interests, not in the interest of a financial giant that pays their salary.

INVESTMENT MYTHS

If there is an underlying theme in this book, it's that the stock market, arguably the most powerful device ever invented for growing one's wealth, is full of myths, false promises, and is often misunderstood by investors.

In Chapter 1, I show how stock bubbles have humbled generations of investors and how Newton got caught up in one. In Chapter 2, we see why stock picking, even when done by market experts, almost invariably leads to disappointing results.

Chapters 3 and 4 are about how index fund investing got invented (and laughed at). I show in Chapters 5 and 6 why lawyers, doctors and dentists are often the worst investors and why the news media won't make us rich.

In Chapter 7, I explain how to deal with the inevitable market downturns and crashes.

Chapter 8 is about why investing with the typical financial advisor is a bit like taking a very expensive taxi on a dangerous exotic island, while in Chapter 9 I show you exactly how to invest your money depending on the level of autonomy you want as an investor, and how you can do so ethically and responsibly.

GOOD PRACTICES

No one comes into this world knowing how to invest. Unfortunately, very few leave it having learned to do so.

> "How could I have been such an idiot?" If you've never yelled that sentence at yourself in a fury, you're not an investor.
>
> *Jason Zweig, financial author*

Anyone who wants to lose weight knows not to fill their freezer with frozen pizzas and fries. A person who wants to increase their physical strength and endurance is not going to spend their evenings smoking cigarettes on the couch believing they are getting closer to their goals.

When it comes to financial investments, however, many people do the equivalent of eating junk food in the belief that they are taking care of their health – an illusion maintained by financial institutions and professionals who claim to be good advisors.

Unlike the main principles of nutrition and physical activity, good investment practices are rarely taught in school and are not the subject of extensive government advertising campaigns. This knowledge is rarely passed on to us by our parents, who are often uncomfortable with the subject themselves. The media sometimes offers us good leads, but they get lost in an avalanche of information that is more likely to lead us astray than to bring us closer to our goal.

For most people, the prospect of learning about this subject is as exciting as spending a weekend reading the owner's manual for their vehicle, buried in the back of the glove compartment.

As a result, someone who wants to get rich from their investments may engage in behaviors that impoverish them or, at the very least, deprive them of more generous returns.

Good investment practices have been known for decades. But the transfer of knowledge from researchers to the public has largely not happened. These lessons are at the heart of the book you are holding in your hands (and that I hope is catchier than a Toyota owner's manual!).

"An ignorant mind is precisely not a spotless, empty vessel," wrote the famous psychologist David Dunning, "but one that's filled with the clutter of irrelevant or misleading life experiences, theories, facts, intuitions, strategies, algorithms, heuristics, metaphors, and hunches that regrettably have the look and feel of useful and accurate knowledge."[4]

I can relate to that statement. I didn't feel like I was doing anything wrong when I started investing for a dramatic market decline several years ago. In fact, I would have reacted badly if someone had told me I didn't know what I was doing.

That person would have been right. I didn't know what I was doing.

The Israeli diplomat Abba Eban used to say that "nations and men will always find the right solution after all other solutions have been tried." I have concluded that investors work the same way.

To understand why, let's go to the heart of London, at the beginning of the 18th century, when the most prominent people in society were obsessed with a few pieces of paper.

CHAPTER 1: EXPLOSIONS AND CONTRACTIONS

Thinking is easy.

Acting is difficult.

But the most difficult thing in the world is to act in accordance with one's thinking.

Johann Wolfgang von Goethe, novelist and scientist

"THE MADNESS OF PEOPLE"

SIR ISAAC NEWTON was not going to let the opportunity of a lifetime slip away.

The summer of 1720 was about to begin, and the mercury was over 70 Fahrenheit in the streets of London when Newton, the genius behind the theory of universal gravitation and one of the greatest scientists of all time, decided to invest most of his fortune in shares of the South Sea Company.

Founded nine years earlier by members of the London intelligentsia, the South Sea Company had been given a monopoly by the British government on trade routes to the Spanish colonies in America to transport slaves and gold.

George I, the king of Great Britain at the time, was one of the directors of the company, which inspired confidence in the eyes of investors. In truth, the company was making little profit, but that did not prevent the public from seeing an opportunity to invest in a business that was sure to do well with the expansion of international trade. The subject was so exciting that it monopolized much of the conversation in London.

Sir Isaac Newton had first invested in the shares of the South Sea Company in February 1720. Within a few months, his investments had doubled in value. Convinced that the company was in the grip of a speculative mania, Newton decided to realize his profit and sell his shares on April 19 of the same year.

Far from falling, the price of shares continued to rise. Newton was no longer getting rich, while his friends and acquaintances continued to see their fortunes grow daily.

Two months after selling, Newton abandoned his reserve. On June 14, he decided to invest again by putting most of his money into the company's stock.

In September, a fraud scandal at the South Sea Company erupted, and its shares quickly lost 90% of their value. Many of the company's top executives were imprisoned in the Tower of London, including members of parliament, and they had their assets confiscated. The scandal was so resounding that it plagued the British financial markets and undermined business formation for generations.[5]

By some accounts, Newton lost 20,000 English pounds in the collapse of the South Sea Company, the equivalent of 20 million in today's dollars.[6]

"I can calculate the motions of the heavenly bodies, but not the madness of people," the physicist is claimed to have concluded.

It is said that Newton was so affected by this debacle that, until his death, he was unable to bear the mention of the South Sea Company's name in his presence.

This episode illustrates how even the most rational and brilliant people can succumb to a speculative mania which is only obvious in retrospect.

The South Sea Company's speculative mania was one of the most devastating of its time. But nearly a century earlier, another bubble had hit elsewhere in Europe: the Tulip Crisis.

A BULB FOR A HOUSE

Considered by many historians to be one of the first speculative bubbles in history, the tulip crisis of the 17th century had its origins in the growing interest of the citizens of the Netherlands in gardening. One of the most spectacular and sought-after flowers of the time was the tulip, whose bulbs from Constantinople had the advantage of withstanding the cold winters of northern Europe.

Gradually, tulips began to appear in the gardens of the gentry in Amsterdam and elsewhere. Gardeners began to create hybrid bulbs that produced tulips with brilliant, marbled colors. Merchants published illustrated catalogs that listed the price of bulbs according to the type of tulip.

The growing demand, especially in France, drove up prices, so that a tulip exchange was established in Amsterdam in 1636. The following year, the price of one particularly prized bulb reached the value a modest house. That's when things started to get strange.

In his book *Extraordinary Popular Delusions and the Madness of Crowds*,[7] published in 1841, the Scottish journalist Charles Mackay reports a series of anecdotes from the period.

He tells of a sailor who inadvertently ate what he thought was a small onion left on his captain's desk, not realizing it was a Semper Augustus, a rare tulip bulb "the price of which might have been enough to feed the crew for an entire year." The reckless sailor was reportedly sentenced to prison.

In 1637, bulb prices began to fall when traders were unable to find new buyers willing to pay stratospheric sums. Speculators who had amassed stocks of bulbs were ruined. The collapse of a previously safe investment vehicle shocked the Dutch public.

From railroads to mining companies to real estate to beer to even bicycle manufacturers in the late 19th century, dozens of speculative bubbles have filled the pages of finance books for centuries.

The most important of these, which resulted in the collapse of Wall Street in the fall of 1929 after years of speculation on credit, shattered confidence in the American economy and set off a domino effect that led millions of people to ruin and opened the door to the Great Depression. Companies listed on the New York Stock Exchange lost a staggering 89% of their value in four years. Nearly a century later, this collapse is still a source of great fascination for the world's financial community.

FIVE TRILLION DOLLARS

One of the most recent speculative bubbles took the world by storm at the end of the 20th century: the dot-com bubble.

At that time, investors were scrambling to make investments in technology companies that often had no customers, no products, and whose profit outlook was more than a little cloudy.

I know: I was one of them.

In my early twenties, I worked as a journalist for an outdoor magazine. It was a dream job: I traveled, tested outdoor equipment, and had the opportunity to interview adventure giants – like Sir Edmund Hillary, who was the first, along with Sherpa Tensing Norgay, to conquer Mount Everest; or Reinhold Messner, the first person to climb all 14 peaks over 8,000 meters.

At that time, another passion occupied my mind, sometimes with even more insistence than the world of the outdoors: that of the internet companies.

My boss, Stephane, the magazine's editor-in-chief, and I had started investing in Netgraphe, a young publicly traded Canadian technology company that promised to use the power of the internet to crush the mainstream media.

In a few months, the value of our investments doubled, then tripled. Every morning at 9:30 a.m., when the markets opened, we exchanged a few cries of "Wow!" or "Unbelievable!" from one office to another, unable to contain our delight at the rise in our stocks.

Watching your investments grow in value day by day makes you feel brilliant. After a quick mental calculation, you realize that these new dollars could be used to buy a new bike, pay six months' rent, buy a used car, then a new car...

One of the most quoted figures in the media at the time was Henry Blodget, a then 34-year-old Wall Street analyst who worked in New York for the investment firm Merrill Lynch. Blodget was known for his analysis that the rise of tech companies was just beginning, and would continue for years to come as their profits grew.

Blodget was not naïve: he realized that the craze for these companies was abnormal. His grandfather had made his fortune in the 1920s before losing it all in the crash of 1929 and the Great Depression. With this family history in mind, he asked older colleagues if they thought history would repeat itself, and that a crash like 1929 was possible.

"Almost to a person they would say, 'No, this is different,'" he recalled years later.[8]

Portfolio manager Marc-André Turcot remembers this period. Also in his early twenties, he worked in the call center of the discount brokerage department of a large financial institution. This was before internet trading, and clients had to phone to buy or sell stocks.

"We had so many new clients that people sometimes had to wait an hour on the phone before they could make their transactions," Turcot explained to me, sitting in the loft in Old Montreal where he has his offices. "They were not happy, because the shares of the companies they wanted to buy had increased in value in the meantime. Once, I got on the line and the client was snoring. He had been waiting on the phone so long that he had fallen asleep. I tried to wake him up, but he was sleeping too hard, and I had to hang up."

One of his regular clients was a dentist. "He would tell us, 'I was rushing with my patient because I wanted to do transactions.' It was crazy. People were making so much money in the stock market that their jobs were almost secondary."

However, the overheated market began to fall when speculators refused to pay more for the shares of tech companies. With no takers, sellers were forced to lower their prices, triggering a cycle of panic.

From its peak in March 2000, the New York-based Nasdaq stock exchange, where the largest technology companies trade, had lost 75% of its value two years later. Pets.com, a company that sold pet products online, saw its stock value drop from $14 to $0.19. A young internet company called Amazon was almost wiped off the map, losing 90% of its value in two years.

Approximately $5 trillion in market value evaporated in the bursting of the bubble. For comparison, this is more than a third of the size of the U.S. economy at the time.

Turcot remembers the stock market crash as a period of silence: "It became very quiet at work because clients stopped calling. They were waiting for the market to rebound."

One of the regulars was a very nice man, always courteous, he recalls. "His portfolio was worth over a million dollars.

He didn't call for months. When he called back, it was worth $70,000. We were seeing tons of stories like that. It was sad."

That's when my boss and I sold our investments. Not at the top, but not at the bottom either. My boss used his profit to renovate his house. Mine was spent on a computer and other equipment.

My experience with the tech bubble gave me the impression that the stock market was a casino. "Very little for me," I said to myself.

For 10 years, I didn't invest a penny.

"PLAYING" IN THE STOCK MARKET

The experiences we have with the stock market in our youth can define our idea of it for the rest of our lives.

Watching your uncle lose his retirement fund in the dot-com bubble implosion of the early 2000s may have scared you so much that you never wanted to "play" the stock market.

Or maybe you remember the dramatic drop in the markets at the beginning of the COVID-19 pandemic. On some days, they lost 11% of their value by lunchtime – a collapse so great that you have to go back to the 1930s to find a point of comparison.

Between 1968 and 1985, the stock markets hardly rose in value. In the 1990s, they only went up. In the 2000s, they experienced crash after crash. In the 2010s, they took off like a rocket, only to fall sharply (and temporarily) in 2020, during the COVID-19 crisis. And then in 2022 they fell again.

All this market volatility can obscure one truth: the stock market has provided generous returns for generations – even after accounting for bubbles, declines, and crashes.

The Dow Jones, an oft-cited stock market index that measures the performance of 30 major U.S. companies, began the 20th century with a value of 66, and ended it with a value of 11,497.

If we include in our calculation the reinvestment of dividends, the portion of corporate profits returned in cash to shareholders usually two or four times per year, $1 invested in the largest U.S. companies at the beginning of the 20th century was worth more than $18,500 a century later.

How can we have a bad experience investing in a market that has turned $1 into $18,500?

By succumbing to the traps that the market sets for us.

We do as Sir Isaac Newton did and find an extraordinary company that will "definitely" make us rich. Or we hear a glowing expert say that a sharp decline is imminent, and we sell our investments while we "ride out the storm."

We wait for a crash before investing. We invest with our bank or financial institution, not realizing that their interests can conflict with ours.

The fascinating thing about the behaviors that impoverish us is that the behaviors don't change. Generations come and go. Behaviors stay.

Yet, investing well can be extremely simple.

Imagine parents investing a dollar a day on behalf of their newborn child in the U.S. stock market.

At age 20, the child takes over, and invests the dollar daily throughout his or her life.

How much would their investments be worth at age 65 if they were to earn the historical return of the U.S. stock market, which is 11.8% per year? They would total $4.8 million.

Now, imagine that for their second child, the parents didn't invest that daily dollar from birth, but that child starts to do so at age 20. How much would he or she have at age 65 if he or she had the same returns on those investments?

The answer: just over $500,000.

This second child would have to invest more than $9 a day starting at age 20 if they wanted to catch up and have $4.8 million by the time they retired.

This is the power of simplicity and time in investment.

This example fascinates me because it is counterintuitive that the earlier start would make so much difference. Waiting to start investing is one of the costliest mistakes you can make.

A CLEAN SLATE

Many argue that the game is already lost, that our emotions condemn us to mediocre returns. It is better to entrust our money to a professional. Let the experts handle it.

I have nothing against using the services of professionals, and I even believe that it is the best solution for most investors. That said, I am proof that it is possible to learn from your mistakes, develop smarter behaviors and invest your own money effortlessly, with less volatility and better returns than professional investors.

Learning to avoid investment pitfalls is also essential, because even if our money is managed by someone else, it's quite possible that we'll make mistakes. That we pay too much in fees. That we sell everything at the worst possible time. That we jump from one investment to the next. That we make a blunder. That we lose our patience.

I would go so far as to say that becoming good investors makes us more complete human beings. At a time when instant reaction is valued more than ever, cultivating the space between what happens to us and how we react to it is one of the most important challenges of our time.

The market has a seemingly endless supply of traps. It uses them one after the other, or at the same time. It makes us feel like geniuses... and then idiots. Its favorite game is to make us suffer one day, to please us the next, to scare us the next month, and so on.

The idea is not to have a perfect record – there is no such thing as a perfect investor. The idea is to avoid the pitfalls.

Let's talk about the first pitfall that investors face: the myth of the rare pearl.

CHAPTER 2:
SEEKING THE
RARE PEARL

Failure is simply the opportunity to begin again, this
time more intelligently.

Henry Ford

O NE OF THE most reputable investors I have had the
chance to meet is Mohnish Pabrai.

Born in 1964 in a working-class district of Mumbai, Mohnish
Pabrai is known for his legendary calm, his salt-and-pepper
moustache reminiscent of that of the maharajas, as well as
for his spectacular results on the stock market.

Growing up, he watched his parents start several businesses,
each of which failed one after the other. "I watched my

parents losing everything multiple times – and when I say losing everything, I mean not having money to buy groceries tomorrow, not having money to pay the rent. The biggest lesson I learned from them is that I didn't see them get rattled."[9]

At the age of 19, Pabrai immigrated to the United States to study computer engineering. In the 1990s, he founded a computer consulting company before selling it for $20 million and attending Harvard Business School. Since then, he has managed his own investment fund on behalf of his clients, with assets of over $500 million.

Mohnish Pabrai made news several years ago when he won the annual auction for a meal with investor Warren Buffett, whom he considers his personal hero. Pabrai and his colleague Guy Spier paid $650,000 for a meal with Buffett, with the money donated to a charity that supports young female entrepreneurs.

A few years ago, I was able to join a group of about ten finance students from the University of California at Los Angeles (UCLA) and spend an afternoon with Pabrai at his offices in Irvine, a city south of Los Angeles. I was excited, as he does not give many interviews.

Pabrai immediately put us at ease. Affable and smiling, obviously happy to share his knowledge and wisdom, he showed us around his premises, including a sunny, impeccably tidy room where he sits to read and reflect. At the corner of a corridor, he also showed us a closed door that led, he said, to a small room where there was a bed.

"It's for napping," he told us. "I take a nap almost every afternoon. I always think better when I have a rested mind."

After spending several hours talking about his career and answering our questions, Mohnish invited us to continue the conversation over a spicy BBQ beef and kimchi dinner at his favorite Korean restaurant.

56%

This is the share of the U.S. stock market in the total value of the world's stock markets.

He told us how market downturns fail to affect him. At the worst of the 2008–2009 crash, for example, the value of the portfolio he manages for his clients fell by 67%. Huge investment banks like Bear Stearns and Lehman Brothers were toppling like dominoes.

"Years later, my wife stumbled across a letter to my investors from 2008," he said. "She was startled when she saw the 67% drop. She said, 'Funny, I didn't notice any change in you that year. You didn't look any different.' Every once in a while, the market goes through a major correction. There's nothing you can do about it. What's the point of panicking?"

The investor also explained how he had managed to achieve spectacular returns in the stock market over the years by building, like Warren Buffett, a portfolio that rarely included more than ten stocks. He studied the financial statements of the companies he was interested in and avoided talking to their managers before deciding to invest, so as not to fall under their spell or fall victim to their sales techniques.

During our meeting, Pabrai became excited as he told us about a company he had just added to his portfolio.

He explained that he had invested millions in shares of Horsehead Holdings, a company specializing in zinc recycling. Zinc was essential to many industrial processes and was increasingly in demand as the global economy expanded.

Based in Pittsburgh, Pennsylvania, Horsehead Holdings was poised for explosive growth, he told us. "They're building a new $500 million state-of-the-art plant – the only one of its kind in North America. They are perfectly positioned to take advantage of the economic recovery."

I was shaken by his presentation. His arguments were so clear and logical that even a child would have trusted him with their piggy bank without hesitation.

"What if I put 20% of my portfolio into this company?" I thought as I drove home that night. "Or better yet, 30%? I could take advantage of this rocket named Horsehead that's about to hit the stratosphere."

I didn't keep in touch with the students I was with that day, so I don't know if any of them invested in the company. I, for one, decided not to.

I didn't regret it. A few years after we met, Horsehead Holdings declared bankruptcy, and its stock market value plummeted by 90%.

THE MYTH OF THE RARE PEARL

Ask a random person to tell you how to invest in the stock market, and you'll get something like, "Well, investors pick the companies they think are the most promising, buy their stock, and hope those companies are the next Apple or Google!"

This is what I call the myth of the rare pearl.

According to this myth, investors have a crystal ball. Those who have the skills to read the future well will be able to find the gem, while the others will fail and must live with the weight of their mistakes.

Maybe people around you have already been victims. Perhaps you have fallen victim to it yourself?

For example, why not invest for the future?

We could try to select the innovations that will mark the next few years, then buy the shares of companies well-positioned to enrich their visionary shareholders. We could choose a small biotech company, an artificial intelligence company, or a company that manufactures lithium batteries, a metal that is increasingly in demand with the rapid growth of electric vehicles.

The problem with this approach to investing is that it has an atrocious track record. Even if we could know today what future world-changing discoveries will be, we are unlikely to get rich on that information.

Let's take one of the most important inventions of all time: the automobile.

The people who invested in a car manufacturer in the early 20th century probably thought they had seen the future. They were right: there are more than 1.4 billion vehicles on the road in the world today.

But investments in automobile manufacturers have generally been financial flops. More than 2,900 car companies have emerged since the turn of the last century in the United States. Nearly all of them have disappeared, swallowed by competitors or, more often, shut down because of insufficient revenues to finance their operations. By the end of the 20th century, only three U.S. automakers were still standing (two of which – GM and Chrysler – were later rescued from bankruptcy by the U.S. federal government during the 2007–2008 economic crisis).

After the automobile, the arrival of aviation revolutionized the way billions of people work and travel. Again, investment in this competitive industry with razor-thin profit margins has rarely yielded the desired results.

Not long ago, it was impossible to talk about stock market investing without someone mentioning cannabis. The soft drug was about to be legalized in my home country, Canada. The stocks of the companies that produced it were skyrocketing in value.

Many people looked at me as if I had two heads when I repeated that these investments had little chance of being successful in the long term. They were convinced that they had found the winning formula to get rich. Everyone knew a neighbor or cousin who had doubled or tripled their money in a few months by investing in this industry.

A share of the multinational cannabis company Tilray was worth over $148 at the time at the Nasdaq stock exchange in New York. A few years later, its value is not enough to deal with an attack of the munchies: it's worth less than $4.

As you can see, it is not so easy to invest for the future by picking out companies that will transform the world.

Even the investments that seem logical and guarantee our enrichment often turn out to be disappointing.

At the beginning of the COVID-19 pandemic, as panic spread around the world, no one knew if a vaccine could be developed, let alone manufactured in sufficient quantities to protect entire populations.

Imagine that a visionary investor foresaw that a multinational pharmaceutical company, say Pfizer, would be able to produce a vaccine in record time – which is what happened.

A $10,000 investment in Pfizer stock in the early days of the pandemic was worth $11,900 a year later, as millions lined up to receive the company's vaccine.

A $10,000 purchase of shares in Starbucks, which had to close hundreds of stores during the pandemic, was worth $14,200 at the end of that same year. That's a 20% better return than Pfizer.

That's why investing can be very, very frustrating.

When it comes to exciting stock market investments, I always have in mind this adage from author Burton Malkiel: "Never buy anything from someone who is out of breath."[10] Warren Buffett says something similar: "Beware the investment activity that produces applause; the great moves are usually greeted by yawns."[11]

Buffett notes that away from the happy hour conversations, media radar and recommendations of the moment, unexciting companies can grow dramatically in the stock market.

In the mid-2000s, Domino's Pizza went public on the New York Stock Exchange. Since then, it has experienced one of the best stock market growths in decades: $10,000 invested in Domino's Pizza shares at the beginning was worth more than $370,000 fifteen years later.

Imagine if we could ride a time machine back to the day of Domino's IPO (initial public offering) with this information. "I know what you should invest in," we would tell our family and friends. "You need to buy Domino's Pizza stock!"

We would probably have been laughed at.

Investors don't want to hear about pizza. They want biotech, lithium, and cannabis stocks.

And they get the results that go with it.

WHAT ABOUT THE PROFESSIONALS?

Are professional investors able to achieve stunning long-term returns in the markets?

In almost all cases, no. And I have the numbers to prove it.

Twice a year for more than 20 years, New York-based financial information firm S&P Global has published its much-anticipated S&P Indices Versus Active report, better known as SPIVA.

The SPIVA reports measure the performance of active managers against the performance of the overall stock market in the U.S. and around the world. In short, this report card allows us to see if professional investors can find the famous gems before anyone else and build portfolios that generate profits faster than the overall market. It's like their report card, handed out on the last day of school before summer vacation.

This report is interesting because it is neutral, and it compares apples to apples. It is easily found on the internet, but I doubt that many professionals mention it when they meet clients.

SPIVA's mid-year 2022 report shows that 55% of professionally managed U.S. large-cap equity funds underperformed the S&P 500 over the past year, 86% underperformed over the past three years, and 90% underperformed over the last decade.[12] Results are similar for mid-cap and small cap funds and are worse for growth funds which, as their name suggests, are supposed to deliver... growth.

DECODING THE S&P 500

I have tried to banish the use of alphabet soup financial jargon in this book, but I cannot avoid it entirely. Let me be brief.

When I talk about the performance of the U.S. stock market, I'm referring to the performance of the S&P 500 index, the most authoritative index. This index represents the 500 largest U.S. companies listed on the New York Stock Exchange and the Nasdaq Stock Market (also located in New York and where technology companies such as Apple and Google are traded). The returns on the S&P 500 have been striking: taking into account crashes, market storms, corrections and other unpleasant events, the value of these 500 companies has increased by an average of almost 12% per year since 1957. For example, $1,000 invested in 1957 in the S&P 500 Index was worth nearly $1.5 million at the time of writing. Yes, you read that correctly.

To invest money in this index, you must go through a financial products firm. These firms offer funds called index funds containing the shares of the companies that make up the S&P 500. Index-based Exchange Traded Funds (ETFs) also contain the same stocks, are easily tradeable and typically have extremely low annual fees.

As for "large-cap," "mid-cap" and "small cap," these refer to the size of the companies in the funds. Large-cap companies have a market capitalization value of over $10 billion, while mid-cap have a value between $2 and $10 billion, and small cap have a market value of $300 million to $2 billion.

These data show that fewer than one in ten professionally managed funds can grow their investments at a faster rate than the stock market over the long term. Note that these are funds managed by experts – people who have studied in this field, who dedicate their careers to it, and who have access to networks and resources that are not available to private individuals.

Some portfolio managers, including Mohnish Pabrai, have been successfully beating the market for years. Some will continue their spectacular run. Others will see their returns decline. Still others will experience epic underperformance.

I don't know if Pabrai lost much money in the collapse of Horsehead Holdings, but I doubt it. He probably had no more than 10% of his assets invested in the company, a strategy that allows him to avoid catastrophic losses. Perhaps he had also sold his investments before the stock collapsed, decimated by the fall in the price of zinc and problems with the construction of the plant.

I only know that if I had been enchanted by this rare pearl, I would be poorer today.

YOUNG PEOPLE SAVE, BUT INVEST LITTLE

Young adults aged 18 to 34 are less likely than others to invest: four-in-five save money, but only one-in-two invest in the capital markets, according to an Ontario Securities Commission study.[13] Among this cohort, 68% say they have other financial priorities, 66% say they do not have enough savings, 59% cite a lack of investment knowledge and 57% fear losing money in the markets.

IS THE *CAISSE* BEATING THE MARKET?

But what about the returns of institutional investors, those gigantic and admired firms that are masters in the art of recruiting the best graduates from the greatest universities, and that have powerful research and analysis tools coupled with phenomenal investment power?

Take the *Caisse de dépôt et placement du Québec* (CDPQ). With more than 850 employees and an imposing steel and glass head office in downtown Montreal, the CDPQ manages more than USD $285 billion in assets, making it one of the largest pension funds in the world.

The CDPQ has an impressive track record. During its first 55 years of existence, from 1965 to 2020, it has averaged an annual return of 8.5%.[14] This means that $10,000 invested with the CDPQ in 1965 was worth over $880,000 55 years later.

A growth that seems staggering, exceptional... until you compare it to that of the stock market indices.

Between 1965 and 2020, a diversified balanced portfolio with 60% U.S., European and emerging market stocks, and 40% bonds (bonds will be discussed in Chapter 4) would have left the CDPQ in the dust: a $10,000 investment would be worth $1.6 million today.

My example is not meant to criticize the CDPQ, which has all sorts of restrictions on how it invests. Rather, it is meant to show that stock market indices are very, very hard to beat.

The CDPQ is in excellent company. Endowment funds of the largest universities in the U.S. also struggle to beat market returns.

According to the National Association of College and University Business Officers (NACUBO), universities with more than one billion dollars in their endowment fund have had annual returns of 8.9% on average over the last 10 years. The S&P 500 returned 13% per year on average over the same period, while a more conservative 75% stocks and 25% bonds portfolio has returned over 10% per year on average.

Even Princeton University's fund, often cited as one of the best performing endowments in recent memory, and whose managers implement an aggressive, equity-biased approach, has returned 10.6% per year on average over the last decade, which is less than the S&P 500.

Even Princeton University's fund, the best performing endowment in recent years, would have turned $10,000 into just under $22,000 in 10 years, a shortfall of nearly 4,000 compared to a balanced portfolio.

Why do endowments at prestigious universities achieve such results?

To justify their huge salaries and enviable benefits, management teams must generate ideas, conduct research and ultimately propose bold investments.

INVEST ALL AT ONCE OR MAKE PERIODIC PURCHASES?

You have received an inheritance or other large sum of money and are wondering if it's better to invest it all at once or divide it up and invest it gradually?

The history of the last 150 years tells us that North American markets go up about two years out of three. Statistically, the more time your dollar spends in the markets, the more likely it is to grow. So, the answer to this dilemma is to invest the amount in one fell swoop... keeping in mind that the market can go down at any time.

If you're not comfortable with the idea of investing all at once, you can set up a simple system to make incremental investments (for example, invest 25% of the amount on the first of each month for four months).

Some will pay off, some will not. And some choices will be downright disastrous. A few years ago, Harvard University's endowment fund bought farmland around the world. Harvard's farmland investments "resulted in windfall remunerations for its fund managers and business partners but have failed as an investment strategy for the university," according to an in-dept report of the strategy.[15] Criticized in the public arena, the fund lost more than $1 billion in the process.

Harvard managers are not incompetent. On the contrary, they are among the best. But even the best investors rarely beat market returns for more than a few consecutive years.

S&P Global data seems to confirm this: over the 10-year period ending on December 31, 2021, 83% of institutional investors underperformed the S&P 500 after fees are deducted.[16]

KINGS OF WALL STREET

Almost all professionals and institutional investors can't beat the long-term market return. But what about the kings of Wall Street?

These multi-millionaires and multi-billionaires whose mission on Earth is to offer an explosive and enviable return to their wealthy clients must surely have a magic touch. If not, why invest with them?

I am talking about the people who run hedge funds, which are funds that can invest in all sorts of assets and strategies. Equities, land, private companies, currencies, metals, whatever: their only objective is to maximize returns while limiting losses.

After his studies in finance, management and engineering, Ian Gascon, portfolio manager and president of Idema Investments, was able to personally meet many of these investors in New York. He was then working at a large financial institution where he oversaw institutional portfolio management.

"I had to study their strategies, their ways of investing," Gascon explained in an interview. "I finally realized that most of these wonderful managers, the most sophisticated people on the planet in terms of portfolio management, people who make millions, if not billions, were adding very little long-term value. They were essentially running a big marketing machine."

This story reminds me of New York-based manager David Einhorn. Starting from scratch, Einhorn had tremendous success in the early 2000s, averaging 26% returns per year for a decade with his firm Greenlight Capital.

That kind of performance attracts attention: his investment talent made him a celebrity. Einhorn became a billionaire in his 40s, even though his cherubic looks made him look 10 years younger. He was named one of *Time* magazine's 100 Most Influential People in the World.

The Wall Steet Journal reported that his clients felt so privileged to have Einhorn handle their money that they turned a blind eye to some of his questionable habits, such as his aloof way of communicating with them, his conflicts with some of the CEOs of companies in which he owned stock, and his nights spent partying in Manhattan.

Then something unexpected happened: Einhorn stopped making money.

Greenlight Capital's assets fell from a reported $12 billion in 2014 to a reported $1.2 billion in 2022, the result of poor performance and client flight.

"[Einhorn] is stubborn," a former client told *The Wall Street Journal*. "He's unable to admit he made a mistake. It drives me crazy."[17] In 2022, Einhorn had an incredible year, so who knows what the future holds for him?

In his book *A Random Walk Down Wall Street*, author and economist Burton Malkiel analyzed the performance of top managers in the United States for decades. He noted that the "king" of one decade – a manager who was adored in the press and coveted by new clients – almost always performed below average in subsequent decades.

Burton Malkiel wrote: "As long as there are averages, some managers will outperform. But good performance in one period does not predict good performance in the next."[18]

BUFFETT'S BET

In the mid-2000s, Warren Buffett made a bet that no financial professional would be able to pick five hedge funds that would beat the S&P 500 index on average over the next 10 years.

One would think that managers would have jumped at the chance to demonstrate their superiority and publicly nail the famous billionaire. But the bet was not popular. Only one investor, Ted Seides of Protégé Partners, raised his hand.

Finally, just under 10 years later, Seides conceded defeat. The funds he had carefully chosen to beat the market had risen by just 2.2% per year, compared to a rise of more than 7% a year for the S&P 500. The proceeds from the bet were donated to charity.

And it's not that Seides just had bad luck. Between 1994 and 2021, hedge fund managers collectively have been unable to beat the S&P 500 index, as calculated by Credit Suisse by analyzing 9,000 funds with a minimum of $50 million in assets.

Ten thousand dollars invested in 1994 in these funds would be worth $59,000 today, compared to $135,000 if it had simply been invested in the S&P 500.[19]

What accounts for these poor returns of hedge funds?

The dirty little secret about hedge funds is that the vast majority are closed after a few years, often after suffering catastrophic losses. Researchers who analyzed nearly 6,000 hedge funds over a recent 22-year period realized that barely 1,200 had survived the whole period of the study (the mutual fund industry often does the same thing, closing failing funds – more on that in Chapter 8).[20]

"When trillions of dollars are managed by Wall Streeters charging high fees, it will usually be the managers who reap outsized profits, not the clients," summarized Warren Buffett.[21]

CHOOSING THE WINNERS

The reason that beating the S&P 500 over a long period of time is so difficult is because stocks that perform exceptionally well are rare.

A study by researchers at the University of Arizona of more than 25,000 companies listed on the New York Stock Exchange between 1926 and 2016 shows that just 4% of them were responsible for all the market's gains during that period. The rest of the stocks (96% of the companies) collectively earned zero returns, or negative returns compared to one-month Treasury Bills, which are considered the safest of investments.[22]

"It takes some time to process this paragraph," wrote a humble Thomas Macpherson, managing director and chief investment officer at Nintai Investments LLC, a U.S. investment management firm.

The fact that it's so hard to beat the market goes against all the fundamentals repeated by members of the investment industry, Macpherson noted. "This study was received with all the industry excitement that you might think... Being able to identify the 4% of stocks that will generate long-term gains is extraordinarily difficult."[23]

If I asked you to name the few companies that will provide most of the portfolio growth in the future, which ones would you choose?

There's a good chance that Apple, Google, Microsoft, Tesla or Amazon will be on the list. And that's where the problem lies.

These large companies will likely continue to perform well for years to come. But millions of investors expect them to do well, so their stock price already reflects those expectations.

As a result, their growth tomorrow may be less exciting than their growth yesterday.

Will they be part of the 4% of companies that will be responsible for the rise of the markets in the coming decades? No one knows.

What we do know is that the biggest companies rarely stay on top for long. Take, for example, this list comparing the 10 most valuable companies on the U.S. stock market in 2003 and 2023.

THE LARGEST COMPANIES IN THE S&P 500 INDEX

2003	2023
1. General Electric	1. Apple
2. ExxonMobil	2. Microsoft
3. Microsoft	3. Amazon
4. Citigroup	4. Alphabet (Google) Class A shares
5. Pfizer	5. Berkshire Hathaway Class B shares
6. Johnson & Johnson	6. NVIDIA
7. IBM	7. Tesla
8. Procter & Gamble	8. Alphabet (Google) Class C shares
9. AIG	9. ExxonMobil
10. Wal-Mart	10.UnitedHealth Group

With the exception of Microsoft and ExxonMobil, the must-have companies of 2003 were no longer at the top 20 years later – and 20 years is a short time in an investor's life. General Electric, the largest company in 2003, even flirted with bankruptcy and is now the 85th largest company in the S&P 500.

For this reason, investors should be careful before trying to build a portfolio of "winning" companies. Every era has its winners.

If only it were possible to always bet on the right companies, the ones that make their mark and that everyone seems to do business with... That's what the next chapter is all about.

CHAPTER 3:
OUR FAIR SHARE OF
THE PROFITS

This painting of yours will be like all the other things
you started, it will come to nothing. You are no artist.

H. G. Tersteeg, Dutch art dealer, to Vincent Van Gogh

MAGINE IF YOU could earn money each year by picking
the best cyclists in the world.

The rules of the game state that you can use one of two
strategies.

The first way is to try each year to predict which three
athletes will be on the podium of the Tour de France, the
most difficult and prestigious cycling race. To do your
analysis, you could compare the age of the cyclists, their

results in previous races, whether they are injured or not, their performance in the mountains, and their performance on the flat.

If you are right, you make a killing and multiply your money. If you are wrong and one or more of your three cyclists has a bad race or must give up along the way, or some young unknowns from nowhere finish on the podium, your pile of money goes down.

The second strategy you can use is to ignore all of this and choose each year the peloton of the Tour de France. For those less accustomed to the world of cycling, the peloton is the main bunch of riders in the race. They ride together in a group for aerodynamic and other benefits.

By choosing the whole peloton, you may not have any podium finishers in your group. After all, the winners of the race are those who manage to break away from the peloton.

But you'll automatically have almost all of the world's best riders in your group – the ones who are likely to finish the race at locomotive speed, ahead of virtually all the other competitors, famous or not, who weren't agile, strong, or tenacious enough to be in the peloton. And you don't even have to know the names of the riders in your group: the peloton will always be well positioned. Struggling riders will be dropped by it, while future stars will eventually join it. Many of the athletes who will one day be part of the peloton are not even born yet.

If you pick the peloton, your money grows. It doesn't double overnight. But it grows and will compound over time.

So, which of these two choices would you make? Which one would produce a better track record after 10 years, 20 years, 30 years?

This is a reflection that every investor must make.

When it comes to investing, the first choice is to try to select individual stocks (or to entrust your money to someone who will do it for you). Trying to pick companies that will outperform and be on the podium that year, or that will stand out because of their stability or any other desired characteristic.

The second choice is to bet on the peloton and invest in index funds.

INDEX FUNDS AND ETFS – WORKING HARD FOR INVESTORS

Index funds and exchange-traded funds (ETFs) are funds that hold the shares of hundreds or even thousands of publicly traded companies.

By purchasing these financial products, we become co-owners of each of these companies. Since they operate in different sectors (technology, retail, banking, transportation, etc.), this automatically diversifies our investments, and reduces the risk of being stuck with all our marbles in a company or sector that has a disappointing year or a long-term decline.

By far the most popular index funds are those that track the largest companies in a given stock market. In the U.S., the largest index funds are those that track the flagship index on Wall Street, the S&P 500.

Index funds and ETFs are similar products, but with some key differences. Index funds are priced only once a day, at the end of the trading day, and must be bought through a fund provider like Fidelity or Vanguard. ETFs, on the other hand, trade like a stock. They are priced every second that the market is open and can be bought and sold easily and quickly using a brokerage account.

One of the advantages of index funds and ETFs is that, just like the index they follow, they are regularly updated. For example, a company that is in trouble will see its stock market value decline, it will fall down the S&P 500 list, and eventually it will be removed from the group. This is what happened to motorcycle manufacturer Harley-Davidson, which was hit hard by declining sales.

Conversely, a company that grows year after year – Tesla, for example – increases its market capitalization and will advance to join the S&P 500. In other words, like the Tour de France, the composition of the pack of 500 companies evolves to reflect the state of the race.

Can a company grow phenomenally and outperform the S&P 500? Yes, it can. But to achieve sustainable success by investing in this way, one must be able to accurately select the companies that will deliver these epic performances, which vary from year to year. How will you keep doing that year after year, for decades?

As we saw in the previous chapter, the risks of being wrong in this exercise are high, and the chances of being right are low, which explains why almost all investors are unable to beat the growth of an index fund or ETF.

MUTUAL FUNDS VS. ETFS

Mutual funds pool investors' money and give them ownership of a portion of the assets in the fund. The mutual fund is administered by a manager, possibly affiliated with a bank or other financial institution, who makes individual investment decisions based on various objectives, such as preservation or growth of the money invested.

ETFs, on the other hand, are funds that pool together all the stocks in a given stock market index or a subsection of the market (retail, energy, etc.). They are not actively managed by a manager, and this allows them to charge very low fees.

Another advantage of index funds and ETFs is that their expense ratio – the cost charged annually by the fund provider to the investor – is generally extremely low. This differentiates them, for example, from mutual funds, which contain stocks that are hand-picked by managers.

While mutual funds can have annual fees that are between 0.5% and up to 2.0% of the value of the investment, index funds and ETFs have fees that are generally less than 0.2%, and sometimes as low as 0.03%.

At first glance, paying 1% or 2% in fees may seem reasonable. After all, we pay sales taxes at a higher rate than this on other products that we buy, right? So why should we care about a measly 1% or 2%?

The difference between paying 0.03% and 2% in annual expense ratio is barely noticeable in the early years, but becomes as vast as the Grand Canyon over our investing lifetime. As we will see later in this book, this can easily amount to over 50% of our expected returns over many years of investing – evaporated in fees.

The financial industry's business model is largely based on charging clients various fees through mutual funds. In this light, the arrival of more competitive investment products, such as index funds or ETFs, is sometimes considered as undesirable as a large fly in a glass of pinot noir.

Investment professionals' aversion to index funds is nothing new. In fact, it dates to before they were invented.

A "CRAZY" IDEA

The first person to publicly raise the idea of index funds quickly became the laughing stock of the financial world.

American economist Burton Malkiel was 41 years old in 1973 when he published *A Random Walk Down Wall Street*, a book in which he exposed the ineptitude of professionals in building portfolios of stocks for their clients, attempting to beat market returns – to return to our previous example, trying to select the three cyclists who will finish on the podium of the Tour de France each year.

Malkiel was highly qualified – he held an MBA from Harvard and a PhD in economics from Princeton. He had calculated that the best approach for investors would be to buy a fund that no human would bother putting together. This would be a "passive" fund (the Tour de France peloton), which would simply replicate the composition and performance of major stock market indices, such as the S&P 500. The automated aspect of the operation would allow a very small team to oversee the fund, and thus charge 80%–90% less in annual fees than mutual funds, which are managed by a team of analysts and managers.

As soon as it was released, Malkiel's suggestion was shot down. A Wall Street professional reviewing *A Random Walk Down Wall Street* for the financial magazine *BusinessWeek* wrote that it was the "biggest piece of garbage [he had] ever read."

"The book was not well received in Wall Street," Malkiel recalled years later on the *Animal Spirits* podcast. "My idea was called 'crazy.' [People thought] that obviously you wanted professionals to manage a portfolio."[24]

Two years later, in 1975, John Bogle – a Princeton economics graduate whose parents had lost everything in the Great Depression – created the forerunner of index funds. Offered under the banner of Vanguard, an investment firm that Bogle set up, the fund was simply made up of the 500 companies that made up the S&P 500 index.

Bogle, who was 46 at the time, set a goal of raising $150 million in investments to launch his new fund. Due to a lack of interest, he raised just over $11 million. For years, his fund was called "Bogle's Folly" by mockers.

"It totally failed," recalled Burton Malkiel. "Jack picked up just an enormous amount of criticism. It was a success in that it worked, but it was not a marketing success. It remained a very small fund for a long time."[25]

One of the criticisms often made was that passive investing was "un-American," implying that the American way was for investors to take risks to get exciting results in the stock market, not give up on beating the market before the game even started.

The chairman of U.S. asset management giant Fidelity said he "cannot believe" that most investors would be satisfied with receiving only "average" returns – an analysis fraught with bad faith, since achieving average returns over a long period of time produces an overwhelming enrichment that is virtually impossible to surpass, as we will see.

Bogle, for one, said he wasn't affected by this cold reception to his cherished idea. "The more dissent I got, the more confident I was that I was right," he remembered years later. "I'm that kind of a contrarian person."[26]

It took several years for investors to get interested in index funds. Once they did, they never went back.

Vanguard is now one of the world's largest investment management firms. The company founded by John Bogle manages the equivalent of more than $7 trillion on behalf of 30 million investors in 170 countries.

Its annual revenue is just shy of $7 billion – that's $1 of revenue per $1,000 under management. The company's structure is designed so that any profits are intended to reduce annual fees and thus return to investors' pockets.

"Our task remains: earning our fair share of whatever returns our business enterprises are generous enough to provide in the years to come," wrote Bogle in, *The Little Book of Common Sense Investing*. He continued, "The [...] index fund is the only investment that can guarantee we will achieve this goal."[27]

During his long life, John Bogle, who died in 2019 at the age of 89, often cautioned investors who might be tempted to make changes to their portfolios to make them perform better and allow their money to grow faster.

"Don't think you know more than the market, nobody does," he wrote. "And don't act on insights that you think are your own but are usually shared by millions of others."

Warren Buffett is among Bogle's greatest admirers and never misses an opportunity to point out that he revolutionized the finance industry. "If a statue is ever erected to honor the person who has done the most for American investors, the hands down choice should be Jack Bogle," he once wrote.[28]

Burton Malkiel's *A Random Walk Down Wall Street* is now in its 13th edition. Since its release in 1973, the S&P 500 has risen more than 12,000%, including dividends. An investor who invested $10,000 in a hypothetical fund tracking the S&P 500 on the day the book was launched (when such a fund didn't exist yet) would have a portfolio of $1.2 million today. All this while sitting back and doing nothing but letting the market work for them.

After half a century of helping to popularize passive investing, Burton Malkiel is more convinced than ever that self-directed and professional investors should put their money into these financial products.

"The lower the fees investors pay, the more money they're going to keep in their pockets," Malkiel said. "I'm convinced of that. John Bogle used to say, 'In the investment world, you get what you don't pay for,' and I agree with him more than ever."[29]

GETTING KNOWN

Among the first investors to embrace passive investing as we know it today was a Canadian portfolio manager named Richard Morin.

In 1991, Richard Morin invested in the world's first successful ETF, the Toronto 35 Index Participation Fund, known as TIPs.

More than thirty years later, he still hasn't sold the investment.

"I never sell anything in my portfolio," he explains with a smile.

Tall and thin, with a face with angular features reminiscent of actor Robert Redford, Richard Morin grew up in a Montreal-area suburb. With five children to raise, his parents struggled to cling to the lower echelons of the middle class. His father worked as a manager in a sub-prime lending firm – Household Finance – which has since been bought by HSBC: he lent money to clients that the bank refused.

"My father's typical customer was someone who wanted $200 to buy a television," Morin says. "If he didn't pay it back, the company had to go and repossess the TV. My father hated his job, but it paid the bills, and it gave him a good retirement that allowed him to enjoy life."

While completing his MBA at McGill University, Morin saw an ad on a bulletin board for an internship position at the Montreal Stock Exchange. He applied and was hired.

"I knew nothing about finance. That ad changed my life."

Morin worked for the Montreal Stock Exchange for 11 years. Later, he accepted an offer to run the Mauritius Stock Exchange and set up a regional stock exchange in West Africa, in Abidjan, before accepting the position of CEO of the Pakistan Stock Exchange, where he lived and worked for almost two years.

Out of a population of 210 million people, Pakistan had barely 250,000 investors, Morin realized. From generation to generation, Pakistan's elite appropriated all the wealth.

"The Pakistan Stock Exchange was a huge challenge in terms of investor protection. A handful of brokerage firms dominated the market. Our task was to democratize stock market investing. One of the ways we did that was by launching the first ETF in the country's history and enhancing the investor protection fund."

It was while hiking in the Swiss Alps in the 1990s that Morin had the idea of creating a portfolio management firm that would invest only in index ETFs.

Few people knew about ETFs at the time, and it took him several years to realize his dream.

Richard Morin is now President of Archer Portfolio Management, a firm that uses only index funds and index

ETFs to build diversified, tax-efficient portfolios. With eight advisors, the firm manages $300 million in assets for approximately 700 families.

"Our average client has a portfolio of about $400,000, and we put 100% of it into stock and bond ETFs, based on the profile we determine together," says Morin. "There must be a good fit. Sometimes we politely turn clients away because they have a different vision than we do, and I know they won't be happy with us."

The challenge for firms like Archer, says Morin, is to make themselves known. In an industry that is driven by volume, large financial institutions advertise heavily and capture most of the market.

"The average investor has no idea that firms like ours exist," he says.

ACTIVE VS. PASSIVE MANAGEMENT

Active portfolio management involves human intervention: the investor (or someone acting on his or her behalf) buys and sells stock market investments to achieve a given objective, such as rapid growth, greater stability in market storms, etc.

In passive management, the market is in control: once the portfolio has been chosen, the investor (or the person handling his or her investments) is completely hands-off. Note that owning an index ETF does not necessarily mean passive management: many investors buy and sell ETFs based on what they believe the market will do, a behavior associated with poorer long-term returns.

BREAKTHROUGH

Passive investing through index funds or index ETFs is more popular than ever, and is growing rapidly. From nothing a few decades ago, these products now account for about 50% of total assets under management in the United States, 31% in the U.K., and 13% in Canada.

Why did the U.S. turn the corner before most markets around the world?

Ian Gascon, president of Idema Investments, which manages low-cost exchange-traded fund portfolios for clients, says the biggest barrier to passive investing in many places of the world is market structure.

"In many countries, the investment industry is dominated by large financial institutions that have no interest in having all assets migrate to very low-cost solutions," he explains. "A mutual fund with a 2.5% annual fee is much more profitable for the institution than an ETF that will yield 0.2%, so ETFs tend to be offered less often to clients."

Why does this system persist?

I think most people don't know how or how much they pay their financial advisor or portfolio manager. Many simply don't care.

And even if the average investor were to find out, what could they do? Change institutions, only to find themselves in a similar situation?

I also think things are moving slowly because investors retain a desire to find a very talented professional manager. Someone who will be able to turn lead into gold and beat the major market indices for decades, or protect the portfolio during market downturns. This is not an irrational goal on the part of investors.

And if the professional we're dealing with can convince us to avoid selling our investments during a market storm, or if he or she encourages us to save and invest more, it can give us a big boost.

However, the asset management industry is a master at making us believe they have abilities they do not have and convincing us that they deliver higher returns than they really do (more on this in Chapter 8).

And the sums deducted from our investments by investment managers through fees, often over a period of decades, are increasingly being denounced. They are a legacy of another era, when finance was a boys' club that ran on the lack of choice and financial knowledge of the client.

"The customer is being exploited in our industry, not just by the investment advisors," laments billionaire investor Stephen Jarislowsky in his book *In the Investment Jungle*. "Everyone is out to make as much money as possible at the expense of the client, including charging the highest possible fees. If there were less greed and more professionalism in the industry, everyone would benefit."[30]

ARE INDEX FUNDS DANGEROUS?

Embodying the saying that the best way to kill a dog is to say it has rabies, some financial professionals are warning their clients: stay away from index funds and ETFs, they are so popular they are very risky! They distort the market! They are tools of speculation!

They will point out, for example, that the supply of index funds and ETFs has become dizzying and difficult for the uninitiated to navigate, while avoiding the fact that the process of selecting a fund can be very simple, as explained in Chapter 9.

They go on to insist that some ETFs are "dangerous" because they are built around "leverage" that increases or decreases the market movements. All of this without mentioning that these small, specialized ETFs are only used by a tiny fraction of investors.

Critics in the industry have also said that investing in index funds or ETFs is risky because their value fluctuates rapidly. In some years, funds that track the S&P 500 Index can gain or lose 20% or 30% of their value, or more.

What these critics fail to mention is that these funds are composed of 100% stocks: of course their value will fluctuate! No one would recommend to a conservative investor who fears stock market crashes to invest in a portfolio composed only of stocks: such an investor should have a good part of their assets in bonds, which will be explained in the next chapter.

I can see portfolio managers and investment advisors being restless.

"Sure! Our mutual funds and equity portfolios rarely beat the indices," they say. "But that's not what our clients want! They want to sleep well at night and avoid big losses when the markets start to fall. That's what we excel at."

It's an attractive argument, and the New York-based financial information firm S&P Global first analyzed it a few years ago.

After examining more than 1,000 actively managed mutual funds over a recent 14-year period, the researchers concluded that 80% of U.S. mutual funds and 65% of European mutual funds had experienced more volatility than the market sectors in which they invest.[31] In short, professional investment management firms failed to deliver on this promise.

And if passive investing is so risky and dangerous, you have to believe that the news didn't reach Warren Buffett's ears. The Omaha billionaire famously said that in his will, he instructed his executors to invest most of the funds he would leave to his wife in a Vanguard index fund that tracks the S&P 500.[32]

Whether our investments take the form of mutual funds, index funds or ETFs, they are mostly composed of two major asset classes: stocks and bonds. Acting as the yin and yang of our investment portfolio, these assets have the dual role of making us richer and keeping us sane when a market storm hits.

How much should we have in stocks and in bonds? We'll talk about this in the next chapter.

CHAPTER 4:
STOCKS AND BONDS

Let everything happen to you
beauty and terror
Just keep going
No feeling is final.

Rainer Maria Rilke, Austrian poet and novelist

O N T H E O T H E R end of the phone, a childhood friend
I had lost contact with over the years wanted to
convince me to meet him in a golden skyscraper downtown.

"We'll talk about your finances," he said.

The suggestion made me smile; I had no finances. I was
20 years old, attending college and working part-time at
an outdoor store to pay my rent. My only budget was
for beer.

Freshly hired by an insurance and investment company, my friend was looking to expand his client base. Because I was uncomfortable saying no to him, I accepted his offer.

He was dressed in a suit and tie when he received me a few days later, in a large, deserted conference room filled with the light of the setting sun. "This meeting is absurd," I thought. "*I* should be asking him about his finances, not the other way around."

After an hour of discussion, my friend said, "Nicolas, I think the best thing to do is to open a retirement account. You could contribute $25 a month."

Happy to sense that the meeting was coming to an end, I said yes.

He slid a flyer towards me.

"Which fund do you want to buy? We have a stock fund that…"

I stopped him cold.

"I don't want to lose a penny," I told him. "Not. One. Penny."

So my friend invested my $25 a month in a money market fund, a very safe fund, but with a return so low that it doesn't even match inflation. After the investment firm deducted an annual management fee of 2% of the value of my portfolio, I was getting poorer instead of richer.

I'm glad I opened my account – which I now manage myself. But I realize that at 20 years old, my friend didn't have the knowledge to advise me.

If he had, his answer would have been something like: "Nicolas, you are young. You have maybe 70 years ahead of you. You can afford to ignore the volatility of the stock market because your horizon is so far away. You should mostly invest in stock funds, and add money every month, without paying attention to what the market is doing."

HOW MUCH SHOULD I HAVE SAVED AT MY AGE?

This is a controversial topic, and there are many nuances. A teacher who contributes to a retirement plan is in a much different position than a self-employed worker. The asset management firm Fidelity released the following table that gives an idea of the path forward. To arrive at these numbers, Fidelity assumes that we must save and invest 15% of our income starting at age 25. We also need to factor in the present-day value of our retirement plan when calculating our assets.

HOW MUCH MONEY SHOULD I HAVE SAVED?

AGE (YEARS)	EQUIVALENT OF YOUR ANNUAL SALARY SAVED
30	1×
35	2×
40	3×
45	4×
50	6×
55	7×
60	8×

Source: Fidelity.

HOW TO CALCULATE YOUR NET WORTH?

A person's or household's net worth is simply the value of all their assets minus the value of all their debts. For example, a person who owns a $450,000 house and a $50,000 IRA (so $500,000 in assets), and who has a $275,000 mortgage and $25,000 in consumer debt (so $300,000 in debt) has a net worth of $200,000 ($500,000 − $300,000).

MEDIAN AND AVERAGE HOUSEHOLD NET WORTH IN THE UNITED STATES

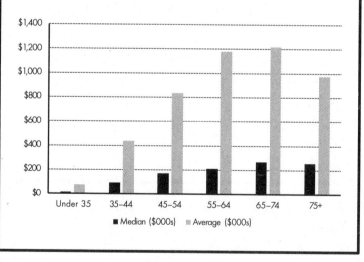

STOCKS

What my friend should have told me is that a balanced portfolio has at least two components: stocks and bonds.

A stock represents an ownership interest in a company. An investor who buys a share of stock owns part of that company. In fact, a portion of the company's profits accrue to them.

The value of a stock reflects the financial condition of the company, and since investors are interested in the future, the stock price takes into account the profit potential of a company in the future.

IN THE MARKET SINCE 1602

Stock markets are often associated with the modern economy, but they were in operation centuries before plastics, transistors, and electricity were invented.

The world's first market where people could buy and sell stocks was founded in Amsterdam in the early 17th century. The first company to operate under these standards was the Dutch East India Company, which would become one of the most powerful trading companies in the world for nearly 200 years.

At the time, shipping between Asia and Europe was lucrative, but risky: the ships that returned generated profits, but many never returned, decimated by storms, disease, or pirates. The idea of founding a stock company was to spread the risk – and the profits – of such voyages among several shareholders.

Dirck van Os, one of Amsterdam's wealthiest merchants, co-founded the company in August 1602. In its first month of existence, 1,143 people became shareholders. At the time, investors went directly to the van Os house, located on a narrow street in what is now Amsterdam's Red Light District, to buy and sell shares in the company. Trading later took place at the brand-new Amsterdam Stock Exchange building. Opened in 1611, it is the first modern stock exchange to incorporate the elements we know today, such as a high volume of daily trading, as well as the freedom to speculate.

It is possible to buy a stock and sell it the same day. Those who do this practice day trading. There are books, courses and seminars about this: a whole online ecosystem exists to teach how to make money by day trading. And you probably have a neighbor or nephew who swears he's going to make a fortune this way.

Unfortunately, studies of day trading conclude that it is riskier than playing roulette at a casino.[33] I think investors should steer clear from day trading at all costs.

Beyond day trading, many people buy stocks to hold them for a few months and then sell them.

But do more frequent transactions increase returns?

On the contrary, they decrease them. Several studies have shown that trading frequency is inversely related to returns. An analysis of more than 65,000 U.S. investors revealed that those who were very active in the markets obtained returns that were half as high as those who were not very active.[34]

In short, as the adage says, our investment portfolio is like a bar of soap: the more we handle it the smaller it gets.

The best way to maximize our returns in the stock market is to let our stocks work for us for years – ideally decades.

Historically, North American and European stock markets are up almost seven years out of ten. Yes, three years out of ten stockholders get poorer. But, over the long term, the odds have been heavily in their favor.

Yet from week to week, month to month, and even year to year, the direction of the market is impossible to predict. The New York Stock Exchange can rise 22% one year, fall 9% the next, rise 14% the year after that, and so on.

WILL THE STOCK MARKET ALWAYS BE ON THE RISE?

Not necessarily. But to expect that the market could enter a permanent state of collapse, one would have to expect, for example, that Starbucks no longer makes a profit selling coffee, that Apple can no longer sell its iPhones, that no one uses Microsoft products or advertises on the internet thanks to Google, or that no one drives a Toyota... It would pretty much mean the end of the world as we know it.

If such a situation were to occur, my priority would probably be to focus on survival, such as gathering firewood to stay warm, rather than worrying about my investment portfolio...

To explain the relationship between the economy and the stock market, investor Ralph Wanger coined the analogy of the master and the dog on a leash.

The story goes like this: imagine that the stock market is like a very excited dog, tied to the end of a long leash held by its owner, and sniffing around in all directions at random.

Imagine that the dog owner, who represents the economy in this example, is walking in New York City from Columbus Circle, through Central Park, to the Metropolitan Museum. From one second to the next, the dog may turn right or left: its movements are impossible to predict with precision.

In the long run, however, its direction is no great mystery: like its owner, the dog is heading northeast at about three miles per hour.

Wanger concludes: "The amazing thing is that almost everyone who follows the market seems to have their eye on the dog, not the owner."[35]

INVESTING YOUR DOWN PAYMENT?

Is it a good idea to invest money that you plan to use as a down payment on a house in the stock market? If you think you'll need to withdraw money in five years or less, you shouldn't invest it. If you do, you run the risk of having to make your withdrawal during or after a market panic, when the value of your investments has declined. With such a short time horizon, it's best to keep the cash in a safe vehicle like a high-interest savings account.

BONDS

Because tolerance for stock market volatility has its limits, a balanced portfolio includes at least one other asset class: bonds.

Buying a bond is no more and no less than lending money to a borrower, either a government or a company, who promises to pay us back in the future, with interest.

In this area, the quality of the borrower is important. The bonds considered to be among the safest are those issued by the U.S. government, or the government of other developed countries. They are considered safe because, unlike corporations, governments have the power to tax, and therefore can collect the money needed to operate.

Bonds generate a fixed income, paid out in the form of cash interest to the bondholder. Since bond prices are impacted by interest rate changes, the most stable bonds are those that represent the shortest duration: for example, those with maturities of one to five years (the best bond ETF choices are discussed in Chapter 9).

Because government bonds are guaranteed by the government, they are less risky, and therefore generally offer lower returns than stocks. For this reason, many investors believe that bonds are useless, that they won't make us rich.

But owning bonds allows us to let our stocks work in peace – that's their greatest benefit.

During a sharp drop in the stock market, "boring" bonds are less likely to fluctuate than stocks, and can help us stay calm by acting as an anchor that stabilizes our boat. They also hold their value and protect our assets during a period of deflation, i.e. when the price of goods decreases, as has happened a few times in the last century.

As the old saying goes, "You buy stocks to eat well; you buy bonds to sleep well."

OUR ROTH IRA NEEDS OUR RESPECT

For some, it's fingernails on a chalkboard that makes them shiver. For others, it's the sound of the dentist's drill. For me, it's hearing a variation on the phrase, "I've been meaning to open a Roth IRA but I haven't found the time."

No. NO! Our Roth IRA should be a top priority, up there with breathing and brushing our teeth. It is our personal tax haven, and we owe it respect.

It's not every day that the federal government allows us to invest up to $6,500, (or $7,500 if you're 50 and older, and with some limits for high earners) by giving us a total and perpetual tax break on the resulting growth (provided we take out the money after the age of 59½).

Once the money is deposited into our Roth IRA account, it's up to us to choose how we want to invest it. We can use it to buy stocks, bonds, ETFs...

The money we take out after the age of 59½ will not be added to our income, and therefore not taxed (there is 10% additional tax if we withdraw the money before that age, in addition to any regular income tax on that amount).

A 20-year-old who puts $5 a day into her Roth IRA, invests it in the U.S. stock market and earns the average historical return would end up with almost $1.5 million, tax-free, at age 60. All this on $5 a day, and nothing else! Granted, few people invest this way – but the purpose of this book is to increase the number of people that do.

Many countries have similar tax-advantaged accounts. In Canada, it's called a Tax-Free Savings Account (TFSA), while the U.K. has the Stocks and Shares ISA. These accounts are even more flexible because investors can choose to withdraw their investment at any time, without paying a penalty.

STOCKS AND BONDS

How to allocate your assets between stocks and bonds?

A good way to prepare your stock and bond portfolio for the inevitable storms is to assess your tolerance for the decline in value of your investments.

This exercise is not perfect, as there is of course a difference between imagining a drop in percentage and experiencing a drop in dollars. The idea of a 20% drop in a $500,000 portfolio may seem tolerable, but seeing the value of that portfolio fall by $100,000 may be alarming, when it's the same thing. An epic stock market drop can also mean the economy is in crisis and our jobs are at risk.

There is probably nothing more stressful than the prospect of seeing our investments and our paycheck disappear at the same time! (Though all is not lost: it was after seeing his substantial employment income from the Paris Stock Exchange disappear in the crash of 1882 that a stockbroker named Paul Gauguin resigned to pursue his new passion, painting.)

In the following table, I show how adding bonds to a portfolio has historically decreased its volatility:

BONDS ALLOCATION AND PORTFOLIO VOLATILITY

I CAN TOLERATE A __% DECLINE IN MY PORTFOLIO IN ORDER TO GENERATE MORE GENEROUS LONG-TERM RETURNS	PERCENTAGE OF MY PORTFOLIO ALLOCATED TO BONDS
40%	10%
35%	20%
30%	30%
25%	40%
20%	50%
15%	60%

In his book *The Little Book of Common Sense Investing*,[36] John Bogle, founder of Vanguard, says a good approach is to start our thinking with a ratio of 50% stocks and 50% bonds. We can then adjust that target to 80/20 in favor of stocks and 20/80 in favor of bonds, depending on whether we're more comfortable with the ups and downs of the markets, or whether we want to prioritize stability.

Specifically, John Bogle suggests an 80/20 stock/bond allocation for younger investors, and 70/30 for mid-career investors. For those entering retirement and beginning to withdraw money from their investments, Bogle suggests a 60/40 allocation for younger retirees, and 50/50 for older retirees.

Also, investors who have an employer-sponsored pension plan must factor this asset into their calculation of acceptable risk. The assurance of receiving payments from this plan in the future removes some of the uncertainty about our future income, and acts much like bonds in a balanced portfolio. This may allow these investors to choose more volatile investments, i.e., to allocate to a higher proportion of stocks.

If you're struggling to choose the stock/bond ratio for your portfolio, fear not: John Bogle, who had a net worth of about $80 million at the end of his life, was also torn on the issue.

"My own total portfolio holds about 50/50 indexed stocks and bonds," he wrote at age 88, a year before his death. "I'm comfortable with that allocation. But I confess that half of the time I worry that I have too much in equities [editor's note: stocks are sometime called equities – in the context of the stock market, the two terms are interchangeable], and the other half of the time that I don't have enough in equities... Finally, we're all just human beings, operating in a fog of ignorance and relying on our circumstances and our common sense to establish an appropriate asset allocation."[37]

CAN I INVEST EVEN IF I HAVE DEBT?

It depends on the type of debt and the interest rate associated with it. Having a reasonable amount of mortgage debt (no more than 2.5 times our annual household income before taxes) should not prevent us from investing. On the other hand, a person who has credit card debt should pay it off before investing, because not only are they not getting rich, they're making the credit card issuer richer by paying them interest.

DO I HAVE TO INVEST IF I CONTRIBUTE TO A RETIREMENT PLAN?

Many people with strong retirement plans, public service workers for example, may wonder if it is necessary to save and invest over and above what is automatically deducted from their pay. The answer to that question is yes, and here's why.

We all know someone who would like to quit their job at 60 (or 55, or 50…) but can't because they are handcuffed by the constraints of their retirement plan. Those who experience this tend not to be very happy with their lot...

On the other hand, if we have saved and invested a portion of our salary over a period of years, and if our investments allow us to do so, we will have the freedom to leave our job when we want to, work part-time, change fields, retire early, etc. Seen in this light, not saving and not investing is more than just passing up a way to get rich: it is letting others determine how we spend our days.

Do you love working so much that the idea of retirement leaves you cold? "No problem!" investor Pete Adeney a.k.a the author behind the popular Mr. Money Mustache blog told me. "Become financially independent anyway. Then you can work purely for fun, and in the process negotiate better terms – not having to attend endless meetings, for example – and devote yourself entirely to what you love about your work."

I am 43 years younger than Bogle was at the end of his life, so I have no problem with experiencing some volatility in stocks. I try to manage my family's assets according to the 75% stocks and 25% bonds formula. I want to increase my likelihood of long-term growth while ensuring that my portfolio retains some of its value when we go through market downturns.

This is not a precise or perfect exercise. The important thing is to find the allocation we are comfortable with.

THE MAP AND
THE TERRITORY

Familiarizing ourselves with the facts so far in this book is important to learning how to invest well. But knowing this information does not automatically make us good investors, just as knowing a map does not make us adventurers.

The problem is that our emotions run wild when it comes to our financial investments. That's what got me interested in investing, and that's what prompted me to write this book.

We think we are talking about money when we talk about investment. In reality, we're talking about doubt, hope, pleasure, regret, fear, other people's opinions, security, ego... That's what makes this subject so fascinating.

The most important aspect of our future returns is undoubtedly our behavior. This is the subject of the following chapters, starting with a seemingly unusual question: why do doctors invest so poorly?

CHAPTER 5:
DRIVING AT 130 MPH
ON THE HIGHWAY

Simplicity can be more difficult than complexity. You have to work hard to clean up your thinking and make it easy.

Steve Jobs, co-founder of Apple

F I WERE to ask you to name some professions that can make you rich, chances are you'd answer "doctor" pretty quickly.

Everyone knows that general practitioners earn a good living, and this is even truer for specialist physicians.

I'll let you in on a secret: many doctors are not rich for all that.

They don't get rich because they are not good investors.

> If you want to see the greatest threat to your financial
> future, go home and take a look in the mirror.
>
> *Jonathan Clements, financial author*

Physicians in the United States, the United Kingdom, Canada, and Australia most often expect to retire around age 60, but actually retire closer to age 69 on average.[38]

One recent study notes that, among other concerns, "financial obligations" are part of the reason they stay on the job. "Personal savings for retirement are more important in medicine than in many other professions, because most doctors are self-employed and will have fewer sources of secure retirement income, such as company pensions."[39]

A doctor friend of mine, whose finances were in trouble after a divorce, once told me that she knew how to invest. "If I really need money," she said, "I'm going to buy stocks in biotech companies. I'm in the business, so it's going to be pretty simple."

I tried to explain to her that speculating in biotech stocks was anything but an investment plan, but nothing helped. She listened politely, but I was far from convincing her.

Financial author and former U.S. securities trader Dan Solin has examined thousands of investment portfolios over his career. "The worst I've seen," he writes, "were those held by doctors and dentists."

Why? Dan Solin notes that the fact that these professionals make a lot of money leads them to believe that they can choose managers who will multiply their savings and take care of funding their retirement.[40]

People who do well in life tend to see the financial markets as instruments that recognize and reward superiority of the investor. "Men are like numbers: they acquire value only by their position," said Napoleon. Having a high-profile position confers all sorts of privileges, but being a good investor isn't one of them.

In fact, very smart people are often bad investors. This phenomenon was studied by financial journalist Eleanor Laise, who for 15 years tracked the stock market returns of the Mensa organization's investment group, whose members have an IQ of 132 or higher, which eliminates 98% of the world's population.

Mensa's brilliant investors who were tasked with selecting great investments earned returns of 2.5% per year on their investments, while the S&P 500 grew by 15.3% per year during the study period.[41]

American billionaire investor Charlie Munger sums it up this way: "I think people have the theory that any intelligent, hard-working person can be a great investor. I think any intelligent person can get to be a pretty good investor and avoid certain obvious traps. But I don't think everybody can be a great investor, or a great chess player."[42]

GET RICH QUICK

However, sometimes investors make good moves, and see the dollars quickly accumulate in their investment account.

That's why I'd like to dedicate this chapter to the best. To those who chose stocks that "beat" the market. Who have managed to turn $15,000 into $45,000, or $150,000 into $450,000, and who didn't wait until they had gray hair to do it.

Thank you for reading this book so far. It can't have been all fun.

If this applies to you then, I suggest, unless you have already done so, that you calculate the performance of your portfolio.

I use the free Portfolio Visualizer site to do this. In the "Backtest Portfolio" section, you can enter the name of the companies you own shares in, choose a start date, and then compare your performance to the benchmarks.

Friends of mine who bought individual stocks and thought they had outperformed the market were surprised when they did this calculation: they may have beaten the market over the short term, but they had underperformed the market over longer time horizons. In their minds they gave disproportionate weight to their good moves, and minimized their average and disastrous moves.

This exercise can highlight an important truth about stock market investing: success is not measured in years. It is calculated in decades.

Most people want to see an immediate increase in the value of their investments. And if you can beat the market in the short term, you conclude that you were "right."

But being successful in investing has nothing to do with being right for a few months, or for a few years.

"To reach your long-term financial goals," writes financial author and *Wall Street Journal* columnist Jason Zweig, "you must be sustainably and reliably right throughout your investing life."

Jason Zweig gives the example of a driver who wants to get to a city 130 miles away. "If I observe the 65-mph speed limit, I'll drive this distance in two hours. But if I go 130 mph, I can get there in just one hour. If I try this and survive, am I 'right'? Should you be tempted to try it too because it 'worked'?"[43]

What Zweig is saying is that investing in promising companies or funds with the goal of an exciting return is a bit like juggling bags of gold and running chainsaws. You feel like you're on top of the world when you grab a bag of gold. But you don't have to think too hard to realize that, sooner or later, the chances are high that you'll end up with the blade of a running chainsaw in the palm of your hand.

INFALLIBLE METHOD

One of the greatest investors of the 20th century was Benjamin Graham. He wrote *The Intelligent Investor*, published in 1949 – a bestseller still popular today and considered the Bible of the investment world. Graham was a professor at Columbia University in New York. One of his brightest students was a young man named Warren Buffett.

One of the investment methods popularized by Benjamin Graham was "cigar butt" investing. The idea was to buy the shares of companies that were out of fashion, had no great prospects, and in which the market had lost interest.

As a result, these stocks were trading at low prices – too low, in fact, in Graham's eyes. His strategy was to buy them for next to nothing, enjoy a little growth, and then sell them. Investing became like picking up cigar butts on the sidewalk. Dirty and uninviting, some of these cigar butts were still good for a puff or two.

The "cigar butt" method was successfully used by Warren Buffett in his early days. But it soon became obsolete: improvement of analysis tools for listed companies meant that the true standing of the company was more likely reflected in the price, and investors stopped using it.

Since then, hundreds of other investment strategies have emerged.

One of them is investing in an IPO, when a promising young company's stock begins to be traded on the market.

These high-profile events often represent an opportunity for company founders to receive millions of dollars for their efforts.

Unfortunately, this excitement rarely translates into attractive gains for investors.

A study on the subject by the American Association of Financial Planners showed that over the long term, IPO companies underperformed the stock market by 2% to 3% per year.[44]

"Buying an IPO is a lot more like playing the lottery than investing in a sure thing," writes David Zuckerman, author of the study. "If your goal is to outperform broad stock market benchmarks, a lot more IPOs will work against you than work for you."[45]

Other methods, such as technical analysis, may seem powerful. This consists of interpreting a series of indicators of a stock with the goal of predicting its direction and being able to profit from it.

According to a study conducted with stock market data from the U.S., U.K., Germany and Italy, technical analysis overall yields worse returns than a randomly selected portfolio of stocks.[46]

Again, the lesson here is that it is dangerous to get too excited about an infallible method of selecting stocks that "beat the market." No selection method is infallible or eternal.

In any case, investing well does not require being very smart. Investing well requires the right behaviors. And one of those behaviors is being patient.

THE SIRENS OF HIGH RETURNS

Around me, I've seen that investors are unpredictable when it comes to letting their investments work in peace.

Some of my friends and relatives could set up a portfolio of index ETFs, add to it regularly with their savings, and that was it. When a big market storm came along, I would ask them how they reacted. "I didn't do anything," they said. "I know it's going down, but I don't pay attention to it."

In other cases, it was more difficult. A friend who had a balanced portfolio of index ETFs couldn't stand to see the value of his account fluctuate while stocks like Apple or Tesla rose dramatically.

Each time I contacted him, he informed me of new decisions he had made regarding his investment portfolio. First, he had transferred it to a high-fee portfolio manager recommended by a friend. Unhappy with the results, he later transferred again, this time to a professional with an even more glittering track record who dealt with high-net-worth clients, some of them very well known. Then, his attention got caught by a "brilliant and Cartesian" friend who was working on programming investment algorithms "capable of generating returns of 10% per month." These algorithms have never materialized to this day.

Will my friend eventually leave his investments alone? No matter how much I deploy logic, arguments and statistics, a new shiny object is always likely to appear, rekindling his hope of a quick and lightning-fast enrichment.

I had a difficult discussion about this same subject with another person I know.

This person was nearly 50 years old, had no retirement plan or real estate, and had saved only $30,000 since the beginning of his career. His goal was to grow that money to achieve financial independence and stop working as soon as possible.

"I understand the benefits of index ETFs and long-term investing," he told me. "But my goal is to get big returns. At my age, with my level of assets, I don't have time to waste. I don't want to see my investments grow by $1,500 a year: I want them to triple. I know that nine out of ten investors fail in beating stock market returns. But, with hard work, my goal is to be in the 10% of investors who succeed."

This person was investing in penny stocks (highly speculative shares of companies trading at $5 or less on the markets) and buying a handful of shares of companies in the hallucinogenic drug business, such as LSD, ketamine, magic mushrooms, and other highly volatile fringe sectors.

This investor had started investing in the stock market three years earlier. After calculating his good and bad moves, he had lost money and experienced extreme stress. During that same period, a diversified portfolio of index ETFs rose in value by 30%.

I sympathize with this investor. Starting to follow the stock market every day, reading different blogs and getting serious about investing feels a bit like standing on the sidewalk and watching a big party through a bar window. The people are beautiful, they have drinks in their hands. Everything seems to be going their way. We want to be part of the festivities. Especially since the party seems to be so close at hand we can almost touch it.

When we decide to enter, however, we realize that we were not in front of a bar window, but in front of the Madison Square Garden hockey rink. Suddenly, the beautiful customers become huge 29-year-old defensemen who skate towards us at full speed to hit us and take the puck away.

With his three years of losses, my harried investor friend was beginning to understand this. But he wanted to keep trying.

"You are chasing a mirage," I said. "Your goal is to get rich, but your behavior is doing everything to keep you from it."

When we start investing later in life, the trap is to try to make up for the years we didn't invest by chasing explosive returns – returns that are impossible to achieve consistently and predictably, and that come with high risks of suffering catastrophic losses.

The person in their 40s or 50s who is starting to invest is at a disadvantage. But they also have some advantages.

People generally earn more at this age than in their 20s, so there is the potential to put more money aside. We may also eventually receive an inheritance when we are later in life (the average middle class inheritance in the United States is over $100,000), which could add to our asset base.

And let's not forget that our investing lives don't end when we turn 65. A 50-year-old could be investing in the markets for 40 years or more.

During our exchange, I suggested to my harried investor that he stop speculating and increase his savings. Invested in a diversified way, this money could work for him for the rest of his life and minimize the risk that he would have regrets about the way he conducted his finances.

He listened to me, but I could see that it wasn't working: the sirens of high returns were taking up all the space in his mind. I ended the conversation by simply wishing him good luck.

BEST PRACTICES

This person's behavior is far from unique. Even investors who are well versed in the history of the stock market, people who already understand and apply the concepts in this book, can deviate from these principles over time.

Personal finance blogger Vincent Morin once explained that he switched to stock picking when he knew full well that his portfolio of index ETFs was much more likely to deliver good long-term returns.

"I had moved away [from index ETFs] for several reasons, including having more 'fun' investing (what a bad reason!) with growth or volatile stocks,"[47] he writes.

Investing this way has given him some quick wins. But he also suffered several losses, "one of which was very large." That shock made him revert to his original strategy. "It's by making mistakes that we learn. Hopefully these mistakes won't be too costly," he said.[48]

The self-analysis that this investor is capable of is impressive. Many people don't do the exercise of calculating how their assets would have performed if they had implemented the best practices instead of trying to beat the market.

Financial writer and investor Andrew Hallam, author of the book *Millionaire Teacher*,[49] realized this several years ago when he decided to sell his entire portfolio worth over $1 million and replace it with a portfolio of index ETFs.

Andrew had built his original stock portfolio after careful – some would say maniacal – analysis, more thorough than many professional managers.

"If I was interested in a business," Andrew writes, "I ordered ten years of annual reports, then read every word, starting with the juicy stuff at the back (lawsuits, back taxes owed, etc.). Data like dividend increases, sales increases, net income levels... they were just a starting point. I took ages to make a stock buying decision, and I typically bought my stocks when nobody else wanted them."[50]

ARE DIVIDENDS FREE MONEY?

Dividends are the portion of a company's profits that are returned to its shareholders at the end of each quarter. We may think of it as "free money" because dividends are given to us in the form of cash that appears in our investment account.

Some investors seem fixated on dividends as a convenient way to earn income without having to sell investments. But dividends don't just fall from the sky. A company that chooses to pay out a portion of its profits to investors is forgoing the use of that money, such as upgrading its equipment or developing new products. By trying to please its shareholders, it could be overtaken by a competitor who would use its profits to improve its offer and would see its stock market value rise to reflect its advantageous prospects. Also, the stock market value of a company tends to fall by an amount of money equivalent to the dividend before it is paid.[51] In the long run, there is no evidence that companies that pay dividends have a higher return than those that do not.

Andrew's portfolio had been growing faster than the stock market indices for several years. But the author concluded that he was mostly very lucky.

"My pride told me to keep the stocks. But my head told me to sell them, in favor of a total stock market index."

After years of thought and hesitation, Andrew made the decision to sell (he was living in Singapore at the time, a country that does not tax capital gains, so the move was less painful to execute).

"When I finally decided to go for it, I had to do it quickly," he notes. "For one week, I felt hollow."

What made him decide to act was the calculation of how much money he was leaving on the table by continuing to hold individual company stocks in his portfolio. If his stocks had underperformed the market indexes by just 1% per year over the next 20 years, his "pride" would have cost him $400,000, the cumulative difference of 1% less per year on his investments for two decades.

To those who say he could have beaten the market by 1% a year and made an extra $400,000, Andrew says the world's greatest portfolio managers would sell both arms to achieve that kind of return. "The odds aren't great," he says.

THE CHIMERA OF THE CAPITAL GAINS TAX

Will we pay tax if we sell stock investments that have appreciated in value?

The amount of tax we pay depends on the type of investment account in which we hold the investment. For example, in an Individual Retirement Account (IRA), the most popular choice for those saving for retirement, tax is only paid when we withdraw the money from our account, provided it's after the age of 59½. The sums withdrawn are then fully added to our income for the current year. In a Roth IRA we pay no tax when we choose to withdraw the money from the account, also provided it's after the age of 59½.

What happens if we sell investments held in a regular investment account for a profit? There is a certain myth surrounding this type of account: we sometimes feel that the governments will eat us alive if we dare to make a dollar profit (called capital gains) on our investments. In reality, our investments are generally tax efficient... provided we are patient.

In the U.S. there are two types of capital gains taxes: short-term and long-term. The short-term capital gains rate applies to financial products we bought and sold within one year. After we sell, any capital gains are simply added to our income for that year.

Long-term capital gains tax rates, on the other hand, apply for investments held for more than a year. The tax rates for those gains can either be 0%, 15% or 20%, depending on our income that year.

For example, a person who gets $2,000 for the sale of an investment that he or she bought for $1,000 and kept for more than a year would realize a capital gain of $1,000; of this amount, that person would pay a maximum federal tax of 20% – that's $200. This investor would get to keep $1,800 out of the $2,000. That's at the federal level: many states tax capital gains, but often at a lower rate than regular income. Some states, including Alaska, Florida, New Hampshire, Nevada, South Dakota, Tennessee, Texas, Washington, and Wyoming, don't tax capital gains.

INFINITE VISION

In his book *The Infinite Game*, author Simon Sinek differentiates between short-term wins in life and the lasting benefits that come from taking the long view, which he calls "infinite vision."

"For all its benefits, acting with an infinite, long-term view is not easy," writes Sinek. "It takes real effort. As human beings, we are naturally inclined to seek out immediate solutions to uncomfortable problems and prioritize quick wins to advance our ambitions. We tend to see the world in terms of successes and failures, winners and losers. This default win-lose mode can sometimes work for the short term; however, it can have grave consequences over the longer term."[52]

Similarly, successful investing also requires a long-term view: in investing, there is often no finish line. Yes, a 60% gain in a few months is exciting. But unless you're on your deathbed, your investment horizon is much longer than a few months.

That's why I never know what to say when people tell me that they've been getting spectacular returns in the market for a few months, or a few years. Or that they've just made a killing with a small company's stock that's gone up.

It's not that aiming for high performance is bad. It's just that achieving explosive performance is a bit like finding a way to get to the front of the race at mile eight of a marathon. Is that really what we're looking for? Our track record as investors will suck if we crash in the middle of the race.

Seeking superior gains in the interest of getting rich quick also causes us to lose sight of a crucial truth that is often misunderstood by even the most experienced investors: achieving an "average" return (in the sense of achieving the market average) does not make us average investors. Maintained over many years, an average return makes us heavyweight investment champions.

At first glance, this statement doesn't make sense. Seeing the value of our investments rise 18% one year, fall 5% the next, and rise 9% the year after that can make it seem like they're not going anywhere.

That's true... at least in the short term.

After 10 or 15 years of investing, something phenomenal starts to happen. The value of our investments growing at an "average" pace now fluctuates by tens of thousands of dollars per year, then per month, then per week, then per day. The market is not moving any more than it did before. But the effect of compound interest is starting to show.

Compound interest is simply interest earned on interest. The resulting increase is not linear, but exponential. The interest we make on an investment accumulates interest, which in turn accumulates interest...

We find ourselves like Jean de Florette, the eponymous hero of the classic French novel by Marcel Pagnol. Jean de Florette, a city dweller who inherits property in a village in Provence, wants to start a rabbit farm.

Ugolin, his neighbor, explains: "If you start with two rabbits, after six months, you have more than a thousand. And if you let it go on, it's perdition, that's how they ate Australia."

We want our dollars to become like the rabbits in *Jean de Florette*. But six months is not enough. We need years to start seeing our rabbits eat Australia – where 13 rabbits introduced for hunting in 1859 have grown to more than 200 million today (the word "interest," by the way, means "offspring" in Greek, the livestock that multiplies with time and births).

BENJAMIN FRANKLIN: OLYMPIAN OF COMPOUND INTEREST

One of the greatest practitioners of the power of compound interest was Benjamin Franklin. A politician, scientist, self-made man, and one of the fathers of the U.S. Constitution, Franklin explained compound interest in these words, "Money makes money. And the money that money makes makes money."

Benjamin Franklin didn't let his own money multiply for 50, 60 or even 70 years, but for 200 years. That's because at the end of his life, Franklin asked that his executors invest £1,000 (or about $200,000 in today's dollars) in an investment fund that would be used to help young skilled workers in Boston and Philadelphia.[53] Franklin wanted these investments to be liquidated in two installments, 100 years and 200 years after his death. Sold in 1890, the first tranche of the funds was used to finance the creation of the Benjamin Franklin Institute of Technology (BFIT), a technical school in Boston now attended by more than 500 students. In 1990, the remaining investments, then worth $6.5 million, were given to The Franklin Institute, a science museum in Philadelphia.[54] This ingenious scheme teaches us that, indeed, money that money makes makes money.

Here is the effect of growing at 10% per year on an initial investment of $10,000. Each line contains the number of years it would take to earn an additional $10,000, the same as our starting amount (amounts are rounded for ease of reading):

$10,000 × 1.1 × 1.1 × 1.1 × 1.1 × 1.1 × 1.1 × 1.1 ≈ $20,000 (7 years)

$20,000 × 1.1 × 1.1 × 1.1 × 1.1 ≈ $30,000 (4 years)

$30,000 × 1.1 × 1.1 × 1.1 ≈ $40,000 (3 years)

$40,000 × 1.1 × 1.1 ≈ $50,000 (2 years)

Using this example, accumulating $10,000 of growth from a $10,000 portfolio takes seven years. But accumulating the same $10,000 of growth when our portfolio is worth $40,000 takes just over two years. Overall, we proceed from a starting amount of $10,000 to $50,000 in 16 years, a total return of 400%.

Our main task as investors is to never lose sight of the fact that it is compound interest that makes us rich, not the few exceptional years that can be obtained if we are in the right place at the right time and have made the right investment choices.

Compound interest needs time to unfold its unique powers. It doesn't take kindly to being interrupted along the way because we want to invest in a small biotech company that is supposed to give us an exciting upside, or because a drop in the market causes us to sell our investments.

One of my favorite studies on the subject was made by the asset management firm Fidelity.

The firm's executives reportedly wanted to know which of their millions of clients had achieved the best long-term returns in terms of investment growth.

The result: the clients who had the best returns were those who had forgotten they had an account with Fidelity.[55]

Compound interest is the foundation upon which our success as investors rests. The prospect of not letting our investments do their work as soon as possible and for as long as possible should scare us.

I'm not saying that we shouldn't spend a penny in our life, and that we'll only be rich when we're old. I believe that throughout one's life, one must achieve a balance between spending on the one hand, and saving and investing on the other. I also believe that, for most of us, this balance is not achieved. All the attention in our society is focused on spending, and very little on saving and investing.

Understanding how compound interest works is one way to rectify this imbalance.

When it comes to wealth, the paths we think are shortcuts are often mirages. The sooner we realize this, the sooner we can join the group of investors who really stand out – those who are not in a hurry.

As Warren Buffett likes to say, "You can't produce a baby in one month by getting nine women pregnant. No matter how great the talent or efforts, some things just take time."

CAN YOU INVEST BEFORE THE AGE OF 18?

To maximize the phenomenon of compound interest, it is beneficial to start investing as young as possible – preferably when a child or teenager. A parent can help their child become an investor by opening a custodial account. Many online brokers offer these accounts, including Charles Schwab, E-Trade and Fidelity, just to name a few. In a custodial account, all assets are held in the child's name, and must be turned over to the child when he or she reaches the age of majority, typically 18, but up to 25, depending on the governing state.

WINNING IN INVESTING

The reason the power of compound interest is so counterintuitive is that time is rarely seen as our ally.

Everything around us seems to lose value and degrade over the years. The incredible computer we acquired a few years ago is starting to slow down. Our house needs expensive maintenance to continue to withstand the elements. Even our bodies wear out. When it comes to investing, the opposite happens. The investment world is one of the few where time is on our side.

I have the impression that the importance of time is often overlooked in investing. In this business, the short term is king. Investors are looking for spectacular returns today – ideally yesterday, in fact.

The irony is that virtually all investors start their careers by buying stocks that they hope will take off in the stock market. It's like a gateway.

That's how portfolio manager Ian Gascon first became interested in the stock market. He was in high school when he decided to buy his first stocks.

"I was fascinated by the idea of being able to make my money work for me," he says. "I opened an account with a discount broker, and I made my mistakes, like everyone else. I was a little naïve... I was buying stocks, but I didn't really know what I was getting into."

In high school, Gascon participated in a stock market simulation contest, which involves managing a fictitious portfolio. A few years later, he won the contest's grand prize. "It gave me the bug."

With a master's degree in finance, a graduate diploma in management, and a bachelor's degree in engineering, Ian Gascon could have made a career out of trying to find stock market investments with spectacular returns. But that's not what he chose.

Instead, he now manages low-cost exchange-traded fund portfolios for his clients.

"The key is not to chase sparkling performances," he concludes. "The key is to stay invested."

"I WAS RIGHT"

Investing is frustrating because we always feel we could have done better. If we invested during a market downturn, and the market goes up quickly, we will be disappointed that we did not invest more. If the market falls after we have invested, we will regret our bad luck and say that we should have waited.

This sentiment is universal. As investors, we need to recognize this. We could always have done better. Even when we're right. Even when we have good returns. We could always have done better.

Investing is almost certain to be a disappointment. At least in the short term.

WHAT IS OPPORTUNITY COST?

Opportunity cost is the financial gain implicitly forgone by making a decision. For example, a person

> who pays $100,000 for a down payment on a condo implicitly forgoes the returns that $100,000 could have generated if invested in the stock market. Or a person who keeps a large amount of cash forgoes the returns that this amount could have generated had it been invested.

If you've been investing for years and buying individual stocks after careful and thorough research, what you're reading here probably doesn't make you scream with joy.

I realize that buying and selling stocks can be exciting for some investors. If this is your case, I suggest you take a small portion of your assets (5% or 10%) and make your trades.

If it helps you let 90% or 95% of your investments grow for decades in index ETFs, this method will have done its job.

Ultimately, the investment world is built on a big misunderstanding, notes financial author Jason Zweig: "If you think investing is exciting, you're not doing it right. Investing should be a mechanical, repetitive process, like a factory that doesn't need human input. Any change we make is almost certainly a mistake. It's hard for people to accept that."[56]

If you can't help but follow the news, believing that being serious about investing requires, at a minimum, absorbing the latest economic data, expert prognostications and market trends, the next chapter is for you.

CHAPTER 6:
TURN OFF THE TV,
SWITCH OFF YOUR
NOTIFICATIONS

The only function of economic forecasting is to make astrology look respectable.

> *John Kenneth Galbraith, economist and*
> *advisor to several American presidents*

HAVE YOU EVER visited the Louvre Museum in Paris?

If so, you have probably taken the time to admire the *Mona Lisa*.

To say that Leonardo da Vinci's 1507 masterpiece is the most famous painting in the world is in itself a cliché. It is also the most expensive: for insurance purposes, it has been valued at nearly one billion dollars. The *Mona Lisa* is literally a crowd pleaser: of the ten million visitors to the Louvre each year, eight million say they go there to gaze at her enigmatic smile.

The Louvre is the world's largest museum of art and antiquities, with over 35,000 objects, but the *Mona Lisa* is the one object most people want to see.

What few people know is that the *Mona Lisa* was not always the star of the Louvre. And that its popularity has its origins in a theft that captivated Europe and the rest of the world a little over a century ago.

On the evening of Sunday, August 20, 1911, three men broke into the Louvre and hid in a closet that contained artists' materials.

The next morning, while the museum was still closed, they unhooked the *Mona Lisa* and removed it from its protective frame before covering it with a blanket and leaving without being spotted.

On that day, the alarm was not given, for the simple reason that no one noticed the painting was missing. It took more than 28 hours for a painter who was finishing a painting of the museum's interior to complain, irritated, about its absence.

The theft of the *Mona Lisa* made headlines around the world.

"Sixty Detectives Seek Stolen 'Mona Lisa'; French Public Outraged," ran the headline in *The New York Times*. When the museum reopened several days later, the public flocked to observe the empty space on the wall where the painting had once hung.

The *Mona Lisa* remained missing for over two years. Finally, one of the three thieves, a man named Vincenzo Perugia, was arrested in Venice after leaving the painting with an art dealer to have it appraised. It turned out the thief knew the *Mona Lisa* well: he was the one who had made the frame covered with glass that was supposed to protect it. He was sentenced to eight months in prison.[57]

No doubt to facilitate its resale, the thieves had targeted a painting of great artistic value, but little known to the public. The story of the theft created such a shockwave in the media that the painting became an overnight centerpiece of the Louvre.

The moral of the *Mona Lisa* theft is that a good story can change the world.

MORE HARM THAN GOOD

If media headlines could create a phenomenon like the *Mona Lisa*, imagine what they can do to the brain of an investor interested in growing their wealth.

Virtually all investors follow the news. The goal is to get a heads up, to be aware of the state of the markets, and to have an idea of what's coming.

Yet, seen through the lens of investment, opening a newspaper, or turning on the TV is more likely to impoverish than enrich us.

If being connected to the latest economic developments made you rich, journalists would be multi-millionaires. Dear reader, I'll let you in on a secret: journalists are not multi-millionaires!

Yes, economic news is interesting, and articles about personal finance can have an impact on our lives.

But as investors, learning that Boeing's orders are in better shape than expected, that Netflix has added five million new subscribers in the European Union over the past three months, or that Apple is struggling to gain a foothold in China is of no use to us.

Those who shout the loudest are often the most wrong. For example, Jim Cramer, star anchor on U.S. financial news channel CNBC, has been making daily recommendations on which stocks to buy and sell based on the state of the market and the economy for over 20 years.

One would expect a man with his expertise and contacts – who seems to be the epitome of Wall Street – to succeed in beating the performance of the S&P 500.

The truth is, he doesn't beat the market. A study a few years ago showed that a fund set up by Jim Cramer had returned 65% over the previous 15 years, compared to 70% for the S&P 500.[58]

So all of Cramer's energy, his thousands of analyses, his countless phone calls to well-placed people, made his investors less wealthy than if they had simply bought an index ETF that tracks the 500 largest companies in the U.S.

As soon as the markets fall, the media goes into disaster mode. We are then bombarded with headlines such as "Bloodbath on Wall Street," "Black day for the markets," or "Three investment ideas to protect your money."

Author and investor Josh Brown has been through many market cycles in his nearly 25-year career. His advice: if you haven't already done so, investors should disable all notifications from news apps on their phone.

"News apps are designed to suck you in from your phone's home screen back into their environment – so that ads can be shown, and your actions can be measured," he writes. "It's not news that matters to you, it's a hook to pull you away from your life and into their trap. Turn that off."[59]

Those who are concerned that their investment performance will suffer are the ones who most need to put their phones down, he adds.

"You will meet zero investors who regularly buy and sell profitably on headline news. Zero. Not even one. It cannot be done. It's a guaranteed money loser. Anyone who doesn't know this yet will know it eventually, when they look back at their results and realize they've beclowned themselves."[60]

In this regard, some of the most insidious articles, in my opinion, are those that explain why a particular company's stock is up or down.

These articles have headlines such as "Bank of America's stock fell today. Here's why," or "Three reasons for Netflix's stock rout."

The tone of these articles often leads us to believe that the authors *knew* that these falls would occur, and that it is a small miracle that they deign to take the keyboard to explain it to us. This helps to reinforce the perception that it is possible to predict these falls. In truth, the authors of these articles had no idea where these stocks were going. They are just trying to find an explanation after the fact to generate clicks from investors.

BAD PREDICTIONS

One of the most perverse effects of the news media is when they make predictions.

Predictions about the markets are a bit like the air we breathe: they exist without us really realizing it. In the newspaper, an expert assures us that "the markets have gone up too much, too fast," and suggests that we invest for a decline. On the news, a columnist says that certain sectors or companies are "due" for an exceptional performance and suggests that we invest accordingly.

These people might not define it in these terms, but what they are doing is simple: they are trying to tell us what the future holds. It's a prediction or a forecast.

If I knew the future of the markets in the short term, I wouldn't waste my time talking about it on television. I would invest every dollar to maximize my returns. To each his own.

Benjamin Graham liked to say that the proliferation of predictions about the future of the markets does not come from the fact that more and more people have a special talent for reading the future. It comes from the fact that millions of investors are burning to know what lies ahead.

"Nearly everyone interested in common stocks wants to be told by someone else what he thinks the market is going to do," he wrote. "The demand being there, it must be supplied."[61]

Graham wasn't impressed by the predictions of experts in his time. But that was decades ago. One would think that predictions have improved since then. That with all the technology and data available to us, the models have become more refined.

Unfortunately, the future is as opaque as ever.

For example, in an analysis by Vanguard a few years ago, they wrote, "For the next few years, our forecast is modest at best. Strong market returns are unlikely over the next five years."[62]

Three years after this prediction was made, the S&P 500 was up over 70%.

Oops.

At the same time, British financial giant Barclays was predicting a 7% rise in the S&P 500 over the next 12 months. In reality, the index rose 21% over that period.

Oops.

A few years ago, business columnist Joe Chidley published in Toronto's *National Post* a column that illustrated – at the author's expense – how risky it is to make predictions about the stock market.

"What smart investors do is forget about what might happen and prepare themselves for whatever may occur, through diversification, reasoned asset allocation and, well, patience," Chidley wrote.[63]

I can only agree with such wisdom. Unfortunately, the columnist did not stop there.

"But the fact is, real investors in the real world don't do that. Let's admit it: there's still an element of instinct, of gut – and, ultimately, of betting – in every decision. For better or for worse," he wrote, hedging his bet by adding that his predictions were "absolutely unguaranteed to actually occur."

The financial columnist then told his readers what his "gut" was telling him: the U.S. stock market had gone up too much, too fast. A long and painful fall was on the menu for the years to come. Chidley ended by saying that, unlike

Wall Street, the Toronto Stock Exchange was a great place to invest in the coming year.

Three years later, U.S. stocks were up 100% – the value of the S&P 500 had doubled. The Canadian stock market, on the other hand, was up three times less than the growth seen in the U.S. in the 12 months following the publication of the column.

Oops.

These bad predictions are more than a series of anecdotes. The U.S. investment research firm CXO Advisory Group analyzed 6,584 predictions about stock market growth made over an eight-year period by 68 experts quoted in the financial pages of major U.S. newspapers.

The analysis showed that the experts were right 47% of the time, less than a coin toss.[64]

Both large and small investors should stick with low-cost index funds.

Warren Buffett

Making fun of bad predictions is easy. What's less funny is that these predictions can influence our behavior.

As we read them, we may be tempted to make changes to our portfolio to reflect what the pros are saying. After all, the experts are highly educated and highly paid. They speak with authority. They must know what they are talking about!

History teaches us that this is not the case.

In an interview, author and investor Andrew Hallam told me that one of the keys to his success in the stock market for more than three decades was that he paid no attention to the warnings of financial professionals, the analyses of economists and the major events that were supposed to move the markets.

"The trick is to learn to ignore the market," Hallam told me. "In the short term, the stock market is like crack: you should never fall under its influence. For the most part, companies will grow their earnings over time, and that's all that matters. It is the systematic aspect of investing that is important. That's why it takes a lot of self-discipline to become a good investor."

Steve Forbes, founder of *Forbes* finance magazine, once said that financial experts know that it is impossible to predict the direction of markets in the short term. But they keep doing it, simply because it's their job.

"In my business, you make more money selling advice than following it," he once said. "That's one of the things we count on in the magazine business – along with the short memory of our readers."[65]

ELECTORAL INVESTMENT

In 2011, during the economic crisis, the polling firm Gallup asked 1,000 adults representative of the U.S. population which investments they thought would see the most growth in the coming years.

Respondents named gold (34%), followed by real estate (19%), then stocks (17%).

A decade later, the results were in: the respondents interviewed by Gallup were terrible investors. Ten thousand dollars invested in gold at the time of that survey was worth just $10,300 after 10 years. The same amount invested in real estate was worth just over $23,000. And $10,000 invested in stocks was worth $38,600.

So, the more unpopular an investment was with the public, the higher its returns proved to be.

In hindsight, the respondents' choices told us more about the concerns of the day than about the future of the markets. At the time the survey was conducted, the U.S. economy was in a near-depression. Stocks had just gone through a few dark years. The public didn't want to hear about them, even though we know today that stocks had tremendous potential.

It is human nature to believe that unloved investments will remain unloved, and that popular investments will remain popular. But the market is not interested in what seems logical, normal, or obvious.

JUST. KEEP. INVESTING.

Warren Buffett once said that even catastrophic events that mark their time, such as wars or pandemics, should not stop us from investing.

In one of his letters to his shareholders, he told of buying his first shares on March 11, 1942, at the age of 11, three months after Japan attacked Pearl Harbor.

To put it mildly, the news was not reassuring in 1942. The U.S. had just joined the Allies, and the war was not going as planned.

Three days before Buffett bought his first stock, *The New York Times* included the headline, "Japanese Smash Bandung Lines." The next day, the newspaper proclaimed, "Japanese Invade New Guinea at 2 Points; Claim Rangoon, and Push West in Burma." The next day: "Foe Clearing Path to Australia; reports 98,000 give up in Java."

Oh yes, and the New York Stock Exchange had just crashed, wiping out all the gains made since the end of the Great Depression.

Rushing into the markets during World War II, Buffett would nevertheless enjoy phenomenal returns for the rest of his life. But if he had been scared by current events, he probably never would have invested.

Some say that the times we live in are more uncertain. That the debt of countries makes economic growth more precarious. That an epic recession or a gigantic political crisis is about to happen.

I would answer that times have always been uncertain. Violent events have always threatened world peace. The risks of recession and depression have always been with us.

Here is a short list of negative events that have occurred in the last decade:

- Russia launches an illegal, large-scale invasion of Ukraine, thousands are killed.

- A deadly insurrection is perpetrated against the Capitol in Washington, D.C.

- The COVID-19 pandemic kills millions of people and causes a stock market crash and a global recession.

- Iranian-backed rebels attack oil refineries in Saudi Arabia.

- The United States declares a trade war on China.

- North Korea conducts a sixth nuclear test.

- Russia illegally interferes in the U.S. presidential election. To everyone's surprise, Donald Trump is elected.

- The European Union refuses Greece's repeated requests for economic aid.

- The European Central Bank adopts a negative interest rate.

- Terrorist attack kills three and injures 280 at the Boston Marathon.

I don't know about you, but just reading this list makes me nervous. Have all these disasters that have monopolized the conversations and front pages of the newspapers scared off investors?

No.

Despite these tragic and dramatic events, a $10,000 investment in U.S. stocks has grown to more than $34,000 over the last decade, an annual return of more than 13%.

Every decade has its crises, its tragedies, its uncertainties. This should not prevent us from investing.

INVESTING IN THE AGE OF GLOBAL WARMING

The issue of global warming is new, unprecedented, and some investors might worry that returns will be disappointing in the future because of this threat.

Several warming scenarios for the coming decades are on the table, and it is unclear how humanity will respond to the risks posed.

U.K.-based international asset management group Schroders has conducted a study on how higher temperatures and more frequent extreme weather events could affect financial markets over the next 30 years.

Their analysis shows that the most economically affected countries could be India, Singapore, and Australia, where market returns are likely to be lower than they would be without the impact of warming.

Other countries may experience the opposite effect. For example, Canada, the U.K., and Switzerland would see an increase in productivity and higher stock market returns over this period than they would have without warming.

"Although this paints a positive picture in these countries for the next 30 years, the longer-term picture is of further increases in temperature and more widespread economic losses," write researchers Craig Botham and Irene Lauro. "The analysis also focuses on economic impact and market returns, not the many other negative side effects of global warming. This is in no way an endorsement of standing still on climate change."[66]

Another study, conducted by the multinational insurance company Swiss Re, also shows that the economies of South and Southeast Asia are particularly vulnerable to the adverse effects of climate change, and that the advanced economies of the northern hemisphere are less vulnerable.[67] If the worst-case scenario of temperature rise were to occur, the size of the global economy would be 18% smaller by mid-century than it would be without warming.[68] Nevertheless, it would be much larger than it is today: there are 7.9 billion people on Earth and, according to the UN, there will be 9.8 billion of us by 2050.

I believe that we must be concerned about climate change, its impact on our planet, and try to fight it to the best of our abilities. In this regard, ejecting

> polluting companies from our portfolio has never been easier, which will be explained in more detail under "Choosing ESG Investing" in Chapter 9.

In terms of our investments, I believe that these fears are not incompatible with long-term investing. We can learn to live with the returns that will be offered to us in the future, even if they are lower than they have been in the past.

DECLINE OF THE WEST

Some critics also claim that the good years of the West are behind us. That the growth experienced in the 20th century cannot continue in the 21st century. That China will dominate the world in the years to come.

The problem with this view is that the decline of the West has been predicted every year for over a century.

In 1918, the German intellectual Oswald Spengler published a bestselling book literally entitled *The Decline of the West*. Let's just say that investors who made investments based on this premise probably did not cover themselves in glory.

I was able to discuss this with financial author and investor Morgan Housel. He agreed, for example, that China will continue to rise in the 21st century. But that doesn't mean that the West will be in for some dark years.

"Ask students graduating from college where they'd rather live – the U.S. or China – and I bet 99% will choose the U.S.," he told me. "This goes beyond language barriers. In terms of purchasing power, adjusted for the cost of living, Americans are still more than five times richer than the Chinese."[69]

The working-age population is already shrinking in China, while it is growing in the United States. And even if economic growth were to be slower in the West, that's still where the innovation is, says Housel.

"On Apple products, it says, 'Designed in California, assembled in China.' Ask students to make a choice between these two stages of manufacturing for their careers. I think you already know the answer."[70]

And those who believe that a country must increase its political and economic influence at all costs to experience an increase in wealth and standard of living should take a look at the United Kingdom.

After centuries of being the dominant political, economic, and military force in the world, the British Empire now exists only in the history books. Yet a $10,000 investment in the U.K.'s largest companies in 1984 was worth nearly $190,000 in 2020, when reinvested dividends are taken into account.

SPECIAL BULLETINS

Studies have shown that negative news affects us more than positive news: our heart rate increases when we hear negative news.

This propensity for humans to pay a lot of attention to negative news is rarely as visible as when it comes to the financial markets.

We all know that the news networks multiply the special bulletins when the stock market falls by a lot in one day. Worried experts then follow one another to try to shed light on this "stock market panic." They talk about retirees, the "big losers of the crisis." They wonder if there will be a "contagion" in the real economy, if a "recession is at our doorstep."

But have you ever seen a special bulletin when the markets go up by a lot? Do we interview the same experts and ask them why the markets are up?

Breathlessly covering stock market panics and ignoring market rallies gives the public the impression that the stock market is a dangerous and fragile mechanism to be wary of. Is it any wonder then that so few people invest, and even fewer invest well?

Stock market crashes are one of my favorite topics in the investment world. They never cease to fascinate me.

How do we keep our cool when the value of our investments is plummeting and our brother-in-law texts us to tell us he's sold everything? That's what we'll see in the next chapter.

CHAPTER 7:
CELEBRATING
STOCK MARKET
CORRECTIONS

Be a long-term optimist who expects the world to fall
to pieces about once a decade.

Morgan Housel, financial author

DURING A THUNDERSTORM on the afternoon of May
10, 1752, a brave volunteer in a sentry box with a metal
rod that rose 40 feet into the sky north of Paris saw a spark
appear before him.

The observation was sensational. The author of the
experiment, Thomas-François Dalibard, had just verified
the hypothesis put forward by Benjamin Franklin that
lightning was an electrical phenomenon.

For thousands of years, humans believed that lightning was a supernatural phenomenon that attested to the wrath of the gods. To appease them, the Greeks and Romans erected temples where lightning had struck the ground.

Later, cities and villages in Europe would ring their bells in the face of an approaching storm to ward off the threat. That succeeded only in endangering the person who climbed the bell tower to operate the bells: during a 35-year period in Germany in the mid-1700s, 386 churches were struck by lightning, and more than 100 bell-ringers were killed. In northern Italy, about 3,000 people were killed in 1769 when lightning struck the church of San Nazaro, detonating the thousands of pounds of gunpowder stored in the basement by the Republic of Venice.[71]

Thanks to Franklin and Dalibard, lightning rods appeared on ships and buildings, ensuring the safety of their occupants during storms. Franklin also created and named the first electrical battery, ushering in an era where electricity had the ability to improve human life.

Lightning bolts are a good starting point for understanding one of the most terrifying phenomena for investors: stock market crashes.

Like lightning, stock market drops can paralyze even the most rational person. Yet, like electricity, they should be celebrated by most of us.

It's a simple lesson, but not an easy one to absorb.

INVESTING WITHOUT PANICKING

I experienced this myself a few years ago when *La Presse*, the newspaper I work for, became a non-profit organization.

My colleagues and I were faced with the choice of leaving our retirement plan money in the hands of the multinational firm that had been managing it up until then, or taking it back and managing it ourselves. Almost all the employees chose the first option.

For my part, I preferred to withdraw the money. I had calculated that even with so-so returns, I would end up with more money and more flexibility than what was being offered by the multinational investment manager.

A colleague also chose this option. He didn't want to manage his own investments, so he withdrew his money and entrusted it to a financial advisor. He soon began tracking his assets daily – something I don't recommend.

As it happened, all of this was taking place during a period of falling stock markets. Stock exchanges around the world were sinking further each day.

At the Christmas party, while a 1980s hit was playing on the dance floor, my colleague tapped me on the shoulder: "I'm already out $15,000!" he said in my ear. He had the look of a guy who was beginning to regret his choice.

A few days later, he came to see me at the office. The stock market had dropped 20% in a few months. "I'd like your advice," he said. "My advisor thinks the market will continue to fall. What do you think?"

I raised my arms in helplessness. "I don't know! The markets can go down another 20%, or they can start going up again tomorrow morning. Nobody has a crystal ball. The best thing to do is nothing."

The markets stopped falling. In the year that followed, stocks rebounded by almost 32%. My colleague was smiling again. And I'm happy to report that he passed his first test. He didn't sell.

Many people think they can handle a stock market crash without panicking. But such an experience does not happen on our phone screen. We feel it in our gut, when we mentally calculate that we have just lost the equivalent of several months, or even several years, of salary.

Humans are all different. Some people won't react to stock market crashes at all. Others will have trouble keeping their cool.

The major financial institutions understand this and offer a wide range of market-linked guaranteed investments to calm the nerves of those who fear volatile markets. These "safer" investments are supposed to offer growth and the assurance that our investments won't melt away in a stock market crash. But they are riddled with constraints, hidden fees, and are very profitable for the institution that sells them.

The selling point that supports these financial products is that stock market crashes are bad and should be avoided at all costs.

For a long time, I subscribed to this view. Seeing the value of my portfolio decline used to trouble me, but I've now done a 180-degree turn on the issue. Today, I'm more interested in the weather tomorrow than in whether the value of my investments is going up or down.

The importance of learning how to react to market downturns cannot be overstated. It is not possible to invest well without being comfortable with the volatile nature of the stock market.

COMMON, INEVITABLE, AND NECESSARY

During the COVID-19 market crash in 2020, my investments melted like never before: in a few weeks, a hole equivalent to years of salary appeared in my account. I never thought of selling my investments or lost a minute's sleep. Yet I don't think I have any special gifts or interest in masochism.

How am I able to do this? Because I learned that market crashes are common, inevitable, and necessary.

> Humans can't sit quietly: We're always fretting, always dissatisfied, always trying to make progress, always trying to divine the future.
>
> *Jonathan Clements, financial author*

For example, since the 1920s, the S&P 500, the index on which we have the most complete historical data, has experienced drops of 5% three times per year on average.[72]

Steeper declines are regularly on the menu. For the past 100 years, a 10% decline has occurred approximately every 16 months.

What about a 20% decline? Such a drop has occurred every seven years on average over the past century. And since the 1950s, the S&P 500 has fallen by about 50% three times, or once every 22 years.

The famous "stock market volatility" is so common that it should not surprise us anymore. But it surprises us every time!

The damage caused by falls is usually short-lived. For example, since World War II, it has taken an average of four months for a correction of 20% or less to be resolved, and for the market to continue as before.[73]

And, since 1974, the S&P 500 has risen "an average of more than 8% one month after the bottom of a market correction of 10% or more, and more than 24% one year later," says one study.[74]

Even after the ultimate cataclysm in finance, the stock market crash of 1929, the market took less than a decade to heal. An unlucky investor who invested in the New York Stock Exchange at the peak of 1929 would have recovered all his money by 1936, four and a half years after the market bottomed out. This was made possible by the fact that dividends, the portion of profits that companies give to their shareholders, continued to be paid out during the Great Depression.

THE PRICE OF ADMISSION

The reason corrections hurt so much is that they feel like punishment – like being slapped on the wrist by a strict teacher for doing something wrong.

Market corrections are not punishments. They are a right of entry.

"Market returns are never free and never will be," writes financial author and investor Morgan Housel.

In his book *The Psychology of Money*, Housel notes that market corrections are not a bug in the system. Accepting that your investments will fall in value is the price you pay for growing them over the long term. Without corrections, there is no risk. Without risk, there is no return.

However, our reflex is to seek a painless reward.

As a result, investors "form tricks and strategies to get the return without paying the price. They trade in and out. They attempt to sell before the next recession and buy before the next boom. [It seems] logical. But the Money Gods do not look highly upon those who seek a reward without paying the price.[75] "

Portfolio manager Marc-André Turcot has noticed that successful investors have one thing in common: they don't hesitate to let their money work even when many people around them are panicking.

He draws parallels with entrepreneurs or real estate owners, who are among the most financially successful people in society.

"Entrepreneurs don't wake up every morning looking at how much their business is worth, or how much their buildings are worth," he explains. "They look at their profits, they look at their sales. At the end of the day, that's how they build value. They think long term. Why should it be any different when the company is trading on the stock market? The problem is that in the stock market, people see the price of their investments change every minute, every second, whereas the building and the business, they're not valued every day, so it doesn't play into the emotions."

Experience counts for a lot. The investors who have the most trouble with volatility in the stock market are often those who start investing fairly late in life, and who invest a large amount of money, such as an inheritance, or the money from the sale of their business, notes Turcot.

"They get a significant amount of money, and they invest it all at once. But they have not had time to familiarize themselves with the ups and downs of the market. Every sudden move causes them to panic. That's why I feel like

80% of my job is to manage the psychological side. The numbers, that's 20 percent."

In short, let's earn our success. Let's leave our portfolio alone. The value of our investments will rise. The value of our investments will fall. There's no point in pulling our hair out over it!

Of course, this advice only applies to investors who hold broad market, low-fee index funds or ETFs. These funds contain the stocks of hundreds, if not thousands, of companies. Historically, markets have always found a way to rise. But many individual companies have never recovered, and their stock market value can eventually reach zero. This is one reason why buying individual stocks is riskier than buying the whole market.

PAYING TOO MUCH

In addition to fearing corrections, we are also generally terrified of paying too much for the investments we buy.

This fear can manifest itself when we hesitate to invest because the markets are at all-time highs. "The markets have gone up 31% in the last year," we might say. "This is not the time to invest, everything is way too expensive!"

Some people wait for a market downturn to invest, much like they wait for a sale to buy a TV or a pair of skis at a discount.

I can understand this impulse: like everyone else, I don't like paying full price for everyday items. But what works for a new set of skis does not work for our investments. When it comes to investing, this strategy will make us poorer.

The truth is, reaching a new high is the norm for the stock market, not the exception. So if you delay your investing because the market has had a strong run, or because it's at new highs, you could be delaying for a long time!

The S&P 500 hit a record high once every 20 business days on average since 1928, writes financial writer Ben Carlson.[76]

Between 1926 and 2019, he calculated, the S&P 500 was up nearly three years out of four. The year after a bullish year? The index was up... nearly three years out of four.[77]

After a year that was up more than 10%? In the year following such growth, the S&P 500 was up... nearly three years out of four.

And after a spectacular, absurd, Himalayan rise – say, a 50% rise in 12 months? After such a performance, we are clearly due for a good correction, right?

Well, no. Historically, the return for the year following an incredible year is indeed negative – it averages −1.5%. But after a 50% up year, the average market return three years later is 42%, and 66% five years later. And that doesn't even include dividend payments.

"Predicting the future path of the stock market based on what it has done over the past year is much harder than it sounds," concludes Carlson.[78]

Another way to look at this is to imagine that you toss a coin in the air repeatedly and write down the results, heads or tails, on a piece of paper. You can get tails several times in a row. The fact that you get tails does not mean that you are "due" to get heads. One toss does not affect the next.

In the case of a coin, the odds are 50% to get heads and 50% to get tails. In the case of the stock market, the odds are historically in the investor's favor: as I mentioned earlier, North American stock markets are up almost seven years out of ten.

This lesson is counterintuitive, but markets that are peaking should not keep us from investing.

Yes, declines are to be expected. But consistently predicting their timing and extent is impossible.

529 PLAN: THE ELECTRIC BICYCLE OF INVESTMENT

I get a mixed response when I ask the parents around me if they contribute to their children's qualified tuition plans, also known as a 529 Plan. Some do, some don't, some aren't sure because their spouse is "taking care of it." Yet these same people could talk to me for hours about the technical details of their latest iPhone or the kitchen they just renovated.

Personally, I consider the 529 Plan to be the electric bicycle of investing, because the U.S. federal government helps us propel it by allowing investment to grow tax free when the money is eventually used to pay for "qualified higher education expenses," such as books, housing, etc. Although contributions to a 529 plan are made with after-tax dollars, most states offer state tax deductions for parental contributions. There are no 529 contribution limits, but since contributions are considered gifts for tax purposes, the maximum an individual can give to qualify for the gift tax exclusion is $16,000. College can be expensive, but it can become a bit more bearable if we plan for it in advance and take advantage of the tax-free growth opportunity the government is giving us.

100% SCARY

As investors, we all dream of investing when the market is depressed after a sharp drop.

In practice, it is more complicated.

When you look at a drop on a chart, you see an opportunity to buy stocks at low prices. But when you experience that drop in real life, that feeling evaporates.

You can rationalize past declines because you know how they ended. But it's very difficult to rationalize the dips of the present because they are 100% terrifying. It's like going into a dark cave without a flashlight. What's lurking in the dark? Nobody knows. We feel our way through, as best we can.

Corrections sometimes take place over a period of weeks, or months. It fuels fear, softens our brains, and makes us doubt everything.

In this context, buying financial assets is often the last thing on our mind. Oh yes, and as soon as we make our purchase, the chances are good that its value will drop instantly.

Watching our investments fall the minute after we buy them can feel like we're holding our paycheck over a candle flame. Let's just say it's not very pleasant. It took me almost a decade to get comfortable with these situations.

In the long run, markets have always found a way to make new highs. In the short term, fear is a much more powerful emotion than the desire to make a profit. Keeping a cool head in these moments is the challenge of a lifetime. It is during these times that our balance sheet as investors is at stake.

Author and financial advisor Garth Turner summed up the sentiment this way: "In my 35-year career, I've seen the same movie repeatedly. Market advances are the norm. Market corrections are the exception. The economy expands far more often and substantially than it contracts. Crises are sharp and short. Recessions are rare and always brief."

Investors with a balanced, diversified portfolio should not be seduced by the fear industry, which becomes louder than ever during stock market crashes, Turner writes. He says, "Stop worrying about your money."[79]

Investor and author Howard Marks describes his thought process during major stock market crises this way: "I think you can reduce it to, either the world ends or it doesn't... And if it doesn't end and we didn't buy, then we didn't do our job." He says that makes it "awfully straightforward" what investors should do.[80]

MISSING THE ELEVATOR

When the COVID-19 crisis began, major stock market indices fell sharply. The S&P 500 lost more than 30% of its value in just over a month – its fastest drop of this magnitude ever.

Like millions of investors, I had my eye on the markets. When I had money to invest, I bought ETFs with the knowledge that their value would continue to fall. When I had no money to invest, I did nothing.

At the same time, many of my friends and acquaintances were also at their computers. People who had been investing for years. Sometimes people who had studied finance. Who *worked* in finance.

Shaken by several weeks of plummeting portfolio values, these friends concluded that the correction was just beginning. They decided to sell their investments with the intention of buying them back later at a better price.

At that time, the news was catastrophic. Here are some examples of the headlines one could read:

- Dow drops nearly 3,000 points, as coronavirus collapse continues; worst day since '87 (CNBC).

- California governor issues statewide order to 'stay at home' as coronavirus cases soar (CNBC).

- Trump blames China for coronavirus pandemic: 'The world is paying a very big price for what they did' (CNBC).

- Coronavirus: COVID-19 has killed more people than SARS and MERS combined, despite lower case fatality rate (*British Medical Journal*).

- 780 million people in China are living under travel restrictions due to the coronavirus outbreak (CNN).

- The COVID-19 Recession Will Hit the Middle Class Hard (*Barron's*).

- Global economy already in recession on coronavirus devastation: Reuters poll (Reuters).

I have been following the news for almost 30 years. Except for 9/11, I have never seen so many apocalyptic headlines published simultaneously.

Most readers probably thought that this was the worst time to invest. We now know that this was wrong.

In the year following these frightening headlines, the S&P 500 soared by 70%, a breathtaking performance that no one saw coming.

"On average, the market starts to rally six months before the good news arrives," says portfolio manager Richard Morin. "It usually starts to rebound when the newspapers only publish end-of-the-world news, and that was the case with COVID-19."

My friends bought back their investments in a hurry and missed out on some of the upside. And they were lucky. In every crisis, many investors miss the *entire* rally. The markets move on and resume their rise, while these investors have crystallized their losses. They are then paralyzed, unable to resign themselves to buying back investments that have since appreciated significantly in value.

These lessons are painful and costly.

Holding on to our investments even when they lose value is important because good days come without warning. Over a recent 30-year period in the U.S., almost all the market's gains occurred on just 90 of the 7,500 days the market was open, or just over 1% of the business days, according to a study by University of Michigan professor H. Nejat Seyhun. An investor who missed that 1% of business days because they had pulled their money out of the market would not have made any money during those 30 long years.[81]

Selling in a panic, or in anticipation of a panic, also means that we believe we can predict the future – perhaps the most expensive "gut feeling" an investor can have.

In investing, the best gut feeling to have is no gut feeling at all.

"I never know what markets are doing to do," said Warren Buffett. "In terms of what's going to happen in a day, a week, a month, or a year even... I never felt that I knew it, and I never felt that was important. In 10, or 20, or 30 years, I think stocks will be a lot higher than they are now."[82]

RECORD-BREAKING SUMMITS

In any case, spending our time and energy trying to buy our investments at the best possible price does not produce the spectacular returns we might expect.

Imagine that, by some incredible stroke of luck, a person could buy investments every time they hit their lowest price after a drop.

Financial analyst and author Nick Maggiulli calculated that between 1970 and 2019, the annual return of an extremely lucky person who invested in the market only when it bottomed out after a fall would have been only 0.4% higher than someone who just invested money each month, without worrying about the ups and downs.[83]

So the additional return for timing the market – which essentially means you have a perfectly working crystal ball – is only 0.4%. Most likely, you wouldn't get it right every time and would in fact be worse off than just buying consistently!

When it comes to investing, following our instincts is a mistake. Listening to that little voice in our head that tells us to wait before investing is a mistake. Selling our investments to regain peace of mind is a mistake.

In investment more than anywhere else, our instinct can sink us.

STAYING THE COURSE

All of this is to say that one of the most important rules in investing is to stay the course. Once you've determined your allocation between stocks and bonds, the best thing to do is not try to change things. Add money when we have it. Take it out when we need it. And that's it.

If it's hard to do, it's mostly because we're not equipped to be good investors. The human species has not survived for hundreds of thousands of years on Earth by sitting back during a disaster. When enemies looted our food supply, or fire threatened our family, we responded.

In the investment world, this reflex can only harm us.

Investor and author Patrick O'Shaughnessy summed it up when he said, "Instead of trying to predict what will work, focus on avoiding the common pitfalls."

On a safari in Africa, he recounted on his *Invest Like the Best* podcast, his guide kept telling him to stand still if a lion charged at him because running away increases the risk of being attacked.

"We were told a hundred times not to run when lions charged us," he said. "Each of our guides had been charged more than 50 times... If you don't run, the lion will stop short and not maul you. You just have to have that lesson beat into your brain a hundred times ahead of time because the basic instinct, as is so often the case with investing, is to run."[84]

Seeing our investment portfolio lose value very quickly makes our brains feel like an angry lion is charging at us. Dollars that were ours the day before are no longer in our possession. Every fiber of our being wants to do something – anything! – to eliminate the threat.

As with the lions, the trick is not to fight the danger, but to fight our reflexes.

WHY ARE WOMEN BETTER INVESTORS?

Several studies have shown that women tend to do better in the stock market than men. The reason: they trade less than men and prefer to invest in diversified funds.[85] A study of clients of the British investment firm Hargreaves Lansdown found that women outperformed men by 0.81% annually over a three-year period. If this outperformance were to last for 30 years, it would mean that women would end up with 25% more assets on average than men.[86]

WE ARE PASSENGERS

When I was a university student going home at the end of the day, I had to take the subway for a 14-station ride – and then hop on a regional bus that left every hour and a half. I didn't want to miss it.

Sitting in the subway car, I kept looking at my watch to see if I would make it in time to catch my bus. As the time went on, my stress level increased. It was often at times like this that the subway made endless stops at empty stations. Every second I wasted was soul-crushing. I was going to miss my bus!

Then I realized that my behavior made no sense. I was not the driver of the subway, but the passenger. Spending my time being stressed would not change the outcome. I was either going to catch my bus, or I was going to miss it. Once I was on the subway, there was nothing I could do to change that equation.

All that anxiety coming out of my ears was unnecessary. I remember the liberating feeling I had when I realized this.

As is the case with the subway, we do not drive the financial markets: we are their passengers. The sooner we realize this, the sooner we understand that our emotions and anxiety are counterproductive. They make no sense.

I live on my salary, not on my investments. Would I be as calm when things fall apart if I were retired and needed my investments to pay the bills? I don't know, but as I explained earlier in this book, it is to guard against this risk that retired people who live off their investments have a lower tolerance for volatility, and typically choose to have a higher proportion of bond ETFs in their portfolio.

I also realized that the investor who obsessively tracks the value of his investments is a bit like a skier who would spend his day focusing on the technical details of the ski lifts.

Yes, the lift is essential to skiing. But, like the investment, it is a tool, not an end in itself. Properly executed, it should disappear into the background and be noticed as little as possible.

All this to say that no one controls market downturns. The good news is that it is entirely possible to control our reaction to them.

Market drops are inevitable. Eliminating them is not desirable.

It's simple, but it's not easy.

Charlie Munger summed it up in one of his famous statements: "If investing were easy, everyone would be rich. It's not *supposed* to be easy. Anyone who finds it easy is stupid."

So, should you manage your own investments? Let professionals handle them for you? Let's find out in the next chapter.

CHAPTER 8:
A SMART INVESTOR'S GUIDE TO SELF-DEFENSE

The hardest thing is the decision to act, the rest is just tenacity.

Amelia Earhart, first woman pilot to cross the Atlantic

IMAGINE YOU ARE on a trip to an exotic island. After a long evening of partying from bar to bar with a merry group of locals, everyone goes home and you end up wandering alone on a poorly lit country road. It starts to rain, you are cold and you realize that inexplicably, you are missing a shoe. The few people you meet do not understand you and stare at you.

Suddenly, a cab passes and stops. You tell the driver the name of your hotel, and he nods.

"I can take you there for 50% of your salary for the next 25 years."

"What?" you answer, insulted. "That is way too much!"

"It's up to you," replies the driver. "But all my colleagues – if they ever happen to pass by here and see you – will ask for this fare. And then finding your way back is complicated, and the island is dangerous. If you try to go alone, in my experience, you won't make it. So 50% of your salary is really a bargain."

If true, this story would probably rank among the worst travel scams ever.

Yet, when we invest our money by dealing with a professional, we are usually offered this deal. It is not presented in those terms, of course. And the person presenting it would probably get angry if compared to a cab driver taking advantage of a vulnerable client.

But that's the reality. When we sign off on the agreement that is submitted to us in a sleek office, often with a great espresso in hand, we could be giving up 50% of the potential returns on our investments – and sometimes much more.

This is no accident. Every year, financial institutions and investment management firms spend hundreds of millions of dollars on TV, radio and web advertising to convince us that they have our best interests at heart, that they are our partners, our friends. That it makes sense to invest with them.

Any kind of saving and investing is of course better than not saving and not investing at all. But it's easy to lose sight of the fact that some of the professionals who assemble our asset portfolio are not impartial. The financial products they present to us are designed to ensure a steady stream of money flowing out of our investments, in their direction, to boost the quarterly revenues of the institution to which they are linked.

COLLECTING CUSTOMERS

A few years ago, financial writer and investor Andrew Hallam did a test. He asked five of his neighbors to make appointments with five financial institutions. Once there, they were to ask for a simple portfolio of index ETFs to be built for them.

In 100% of the cases – five times out of five – they were advised against doing so, with the investment managers suggesting instead that they buy mutual funds with a high expense ratio.

In his analysis, Andrew notes that he doesn't think this is the result of a grand conspiracy to deceive the client. It's that the employees seemed unaware of how index ETFs work. And those employees have sales goals to meet –

whether explicit or implicit – and so they must promote the institution's products.

When these issues are raised, investment professionals have a ready answer: they say we would have worse returns without them.

"Investing is a bit like renovating a house," they say. "Some people can do it themselves and save money. But it's usually better to let the experts handle it."

To make their point, they like to cite an analysis by the U.S. financial services firm Dalbar that shows that self-directed investors underperform the funds they own, simply because they speculate and buy and sell at the wrong time.

What they don't say is that *The Wall Street Journal* and several economists question the methodology used by the Dalbar study, which they say inflates the underperformance of independent investors.[87]

But even assuming, as I am prepared to do, that professionals can successfully prevent their clients from making blunders and advise them wisely on tax and other issues, the impact of the money they sometimes take out of their investments is excessive to the point of absurdity.

To use the example of the cab driver on an exotic island: even if that driver was right that you would be safer with him, does that justify demanding 50% of your salary for the next 25 years?

Let's say we have $100,000 in investments in a balanced portfolio, and we add $10,000 per year. And let's say the investment advisor we deal with charges an annual fee of 2%. That 2% fee is typical: in a rare attempt to paint a complete picture of investment expenses, a 2014 *Financial Analysts Journal* analysis found that the average actively managed mutual funds costs investors 2.27% annually, including mutual fund expenses, advisor fees, and costs associated with buying and selling securities owned by the fund.[88]

At the end of 10 years, and assuming a growth of our investments of 6% per year, the impact of the expense ratio will have caused a shortfall of nearly $45,000 in our investment account, an amount that includes the fees charged as well as the growth that we would have obtained on these fees if they had still been in our possession. Our gain will be about $65,000.

After 25 years of saving and investing, the "hole" in our account created by the impact of the management fee will be $310,000, while our gain will be $320,000.

In short, we will have given up almost half of our returns – our "salary" as investors.

And, after 35 years, the shortfall from the 2% annual management fee will be $785,000, while our gain will be $650,000. In short: the fees have won!

Do these amounts capture your attention?

In other words: we provide the money. We take the risk. The professional we deal with provides no money, and takes no risk. But he will potentially extract hundreds of thousands of dollars from this relationship, which often amounts to a few meetings over the years.

Does this seem fair to you?

I have a suggestion for investment professionals who really believe they deserve the money they are getting (and haven't thrown this book out the window yet!): rather than taking a fee directly from investments without many clients noticing, do what lawyers, dentists, or notaries do, and send them an invoice.

For example, you might send a bill payable on receipt of $30,000 to a retired couple every December for managing their $1.5 million portfolio (which equals a 2% management fee).

Good idea, isn't it? No? So we agree on one thing: the current model serves someone, but it's not the customer.

HOW MUCH CAN WE GET FROM OUR INVESTMENTS TO LIVE ON?

More than 25 years ago, a California financial advisor named Bill Bengen wanted to know how much money a person could withdraw from his or her investments each year to live without working. His conclusion: it is possible to withdraw 4% annually from our investments, with an increase to cover inflation, without fear of running out of money for at least 30 years. For example, one could withdraw $40,000 from a $1 million portfolio in the first year, then $40,800 in the second year (if inflation is at 2%), $41,616 in the third year, and so on. Bengen based his scenario on a diversified portfolio of 60% stocks and 40% U.S. bonds, and took into account returns since the 1920s.

A recent revision of his calculation indicates that it is now possible to withdraw 4.5% of our portfolio per year without running out of money. This rule, he notes, is "conservative," meaning it was designed to work even during the worst periods in the history of stock markets. Also, it doesn't take into account our ability to cut back on spending and take less money out of our investments during market crashes – which would allow us to take out more than 4.5% in years when the market isn't in crisis. "It's not a law of nature," Bengen said. "It's based on the data we have. It's empirical. One size doesn't fit all."[89]

One of the biggest proponents of the 4% rule is Peter Adeney, also known as Mr. Money Moustache. Adeney told me an easy way to know if our investments are enough for us to live on is to have a portfolio that represent 25 times our annual expenses. "The lower your expenses, the sooner you can stop working," he says. "A worker who saves 50% of his or her income could retire after 17 years. Save 75% and you're done working after seven years."

A MILLION OR ELSE...

Portfolio manager Marc-André Turcot knows this dynamic well: it has provided him with a salary for years.

The son of a power lineman, Turcot grew up in a middle-class family. There was little talk of money at home; it was in college that he started reading books on the stock market and finance. He never stopped.

"It was love at first sight," he explains.

After studying finance, Turcot was hired by a large financial institution. He became a financial planner.

"I covered 14 bank branches. I fell into the sales world."

Turcot received a base salary of $45,000, plus commissions on the financial products he sold. He was responsible for his own travel expenses.

"My job was to convince a client to transfer his $200,000 from another financial institution to us," he says. "It was all about the new money we were bringing in. There was no incentive to take care of existing clients. I wanted to take care of them, but I didn't have the time. When a banker is responsible for 300 families, it's impossible for him to take care of those people. So he handles emergencies."

Turcot was not allowed to sell index ETFs. His clients were left with high-fee mutual funds in their portfolios. "It wasn't what I wanted for my clients, but my hands were tied."

What did the customers say? They said nothing, because they didn't realize they had inferior products.

"They weren't interested because they didn't see the fee amount. And even when it's listed, it's not the full fee, just a portion. The information was buried in statements that were hard to understand."

CAN AN INDEPENDENT MANAGER MOVE TO THE SEYCHELLES WITH OUR MONEY?

Not if the funds are held with a custodian. Funds and assets administered by fund managers are often held with a custodian: many banks, accounting firms or law firms offer this service. In the U.S., one of the oldest banking institutions, JPMorgan Chase & Co., is also one of its largest custodian banks. In short, the manager takes care of assets selection in our investment account, but he or she does not hold the money and is not authorized to make withdrawals: only the client is authorized to do so.

All of this has real consequences for clients' finances and lives, he says.

"The institution only puts its energy on people who have a million or more. You, as a client, don't know much about it, because none of it is explained... The people who advise you in general, I don't want to be mean, but they don't have much expertise, they're not very well rounded. It's not a nice cocktail. It would be easy to amass a million for retirement, but people amass a fraction of that because they're poorly advised."

The worst part, he says, is that all financial institutions have an ethics manual that employees must sign every year. "The ethics manual says you have to work for your client, advocate for them... But the speech you get every week is, 'How much did you sell? Did you meet your goals?' And then, if there is a problem with an employee, the institution says: 'We have nothing to do with that, we made him sign an ethics manual!' That's the slightly twisted aspect of this field."

Wanting to move on, Turcot then went to work for the full-service brokerage branch of the same financial institution. He was in charge of investing the assets of wealthy clients.

Again, although indirect, the pressure was high to sell the client ever-more expensive financial products. "Our salary was 40% of the fees paid by our clients. So, the more fees, the more we get paid."

In disagreement with this vision, Turcot decided to resign and seek more independence.

He founded his own agency, Demos Family Wealth Management, attached to Raymond James, a large independent asset manager. Turcot now manages approximately $200 million in assets belonging to some 40 families, with a median asset value of about $1 million.

Turcot does not use any mutual funds in his clients' portfolios: he chooses the stocks of the companies in which he invests for the long term, makes very few transactions afterwards and keeps the fees low for his clients. "We have a portfolio of about 30 stocks and bonds. That's it."

THE ART OF OPACITY

Marc-André Turcot's experience is far from unique. Independent portfolio managers all have "horror stories" to tell.

In a career spanning more than 30 years, manager Richard Morin has seen how financial institutions treat their clients with hidden fees and expensive products.

Financial institutions are masters of opacity, he says. "There are many hidden fees, many layers of fees that are not clearly disclosed in statements. People think they're paying about 1% a year in fees, but they're often paying close to 2%. Over 20, 25 years, the difference is huge."

Morin recalls a couple who came to him several years ago. When he looked at the two retirees' finances, he quickly realized that something was wrong.

"On the advice of their financial institution, this couple kept a $150,000 balance on their line of credit, while at the same time they had an investment portfolio of about $1 million. The institution was earning on both fronts: it was collecting interest on the line of credit and management fees on the million. If the couple sold investments to pay off their line of credit, the bank lost on both sides!"

It's not just banks that take advantage of clients. Morin notes that some investment management firms that claim to have had higher returns than the market for years are "creative" in calculating and publishing those returns.

"For example, some firms only publish returns for a few accounts, which do not reflect the performance of their average client," he says. "Some firms also publish returns from theoretical models (*back-testing*), or returns obtained by the manager before the firm's launch."

WHAT IS THE SECURITIES AND EXCHANGE COMMISSION (SEC)?

The Securities and Exchange Commission (SEC) is the regulatory and supervisory body for the U.S. financial sector. It was created by the U.S. Congress in 1934 as part of Franklin D. Roosevelt's New Deal program, whose goal was in part to prevent another Great Depression. The SEC has a three-part mission:

to protect investors; maintain fair, orderly, and efficient markets; and facilitate capital formation. The SEC receives more than 31,000 complaints and reports of questionable or fraudulent practices per year, according to its most recent annual report. The top three complaints are about cryptocurrency, manipulation of securities/prices, and advance fee fraud. The organization maintains a registry on its website to verify whether the company or person we want to do business with for our investments has the right to engage in activities related to the advice or sale of financial products. It also has an educational mission, and several tools are available on its website, including a demonstration of the impact on investment fees and a compound interest calculator.

Another little secret of the mutual fund industry: poorly performing funds are often closed, and their assets are merged with those of other funds. Their poor track record is erased. This regular housecleaning allows mutual fund providers to boast that their returns are more attractive than they actually are, notes Morin.

So how do you go about investing? How do you grow your money over time while spending an hour or less a year managing your investments, once the machine is up and running?

Let's go on to the next chapter to find out.

CHAPTER 9:
GROW YOUR WEALTH

T O START INVESTING, I see three choices, which I categorize by the level of autonomy on the part of the investor:

1. discount brokerage (*most autonomy*), where you manage your own investments

2. automated management platforms (*some autonomy*), where most of the investing is done for you, and

3. using the services of a professional (*least autonomy*), where your investments are managed by someone else.

Let's look at each of these in turn.

1. DISCOUNT BROKERAGE

Let's start with the least expensive way to invest when it comes to fees: managing your own investments online in a discount brokerage account.

A discount brokerage account is the platform that allows you to buy financial products, such as index funds, ETFs, stocks, and bonds. In short, it is the starting point for the independent investor.

Virtually every bank or credit union offers a discount brokerage platform, and many financial services companies specialize in discount brokerage. Some of the more popular include Fidelity, Charles Schwab Brokerage, TD Ameritrade, Vanguard brokerage services, E-TRADE, and Robinhood. The account opening process is usually simple and done online.

It is possible to open several accounts at once. You can open an investment account, an IRA, a Roth IRA, and sometimes a 529 Plan. Each of these accounts is like a "box" in which you can put the financial products you want.

IRA OR ROTH IRA?

Is it better to contribute to an IRA or a Roth IRA? For me, it's a bit like choosing between a slice of warm apple pie and caramel ice cream: why not take both?

That said, the answer to this question depends on your personal situation.

Just like in a 401(k), the retirement plan offered by 56% of employers in the U.S., contributions to an IRA are made with pre-tax dollars, meaning we don't have to pay taxes on those dollars in the year they are earned, reducing our tax bill for that year. In retirement, withdrawals will be taxed, hopefully at a lower tax rate. The annual IRA contribution limit in 2023 is $6,500 for people under 50, or $7,500 if you're age 50 or older. This limit is increased periodically to account for inflation.

Roth IRA contributions, on the other hand, are made with after-tax dollars, meaning we don't get to reduce our tax bill in the year the contribution is made. The Roth IRA allows the money invested in it ($6,500 per year as a maximum, or $7,500 if you're age 50 or older) to grow tax-free, and the amounts that we withdraw from it after the age of 59½ will never be taxed. Logically, a Roth IRA is an ideal retirement savings account if we're in a lower tax bracket now than we expect to be in during retirement.

And, unlike an IRA, where minimum withdrawals usually must be made when we reach the age of 72, a Roth IRA can continue to grow tax free for our beneficiaries.

> In short, an IRA and a Roth IRA offer a great mix of tax savings, giving us some of the relief now and some in the future.

When the account is open, we can transfer money to it from a checking account.

We can also transfer investments that we have at another institution. To do this, we don't need to have an awkward discussion with the manager or advisor you want to leave: in most cases, we just need to fill out a Transfer Initiation Form (TIF) provided by our discount brokerage platform. I transferred many accounts this way over the years. I didn't have to talk to anyone, and it went smoothly each time.

We also can set up automatic fund transfers, such as every payday, so we can invest without noticing it. Automating transfers is by far the easiest way to invest: rather than making multiple decisions throughout the year, we make one decision and that's it.

Brokerage platforms used to charge up to $20 for a transaction to buy or sell an ETF, regardless of the amount invested. There has been a fee war going on for a few years, and these amounts are trending downward, even to zero in some cases.

Doing it all ourselves is not necessarily the cheapest option if we miss out on some of the benefits, such as getting expert advice on the right stock and bond allocation to adopt, or getting the advice of someone comfortable with the ups and downs of the markets who can prevent us from selling everything at the worst possible time. Bad investor behavior is the costliest of all.

One of the benefits of this type of investing through a discount brokerage account is that we keep more of our returns for ourselves. An investor who is indifferent to market downturns and does little trading is the right person to look after their own investments. Once in place, our investments require virtually no attention from us.

The discount brokerage account approach is the option I chose personally. It suits my personality and ensures that my investments will grow and benefit from compounding for decades.

So which funds to buy? That's the million-dollar question.

There are two approaches: buy a few ETFs, or buy one multi-asset ETF, which is an all-in-one solution. You'll notice that I mostly recommend ETFs over index funds at this stage: it's totally debatable, but to me, ETFs are a better solution for most investors because they typically have a lower expense ratio, are extremely tax efficient, and don't have a minimum investment requirement.

ETFs

Buying index ETFs means building a diversified portfolio of stock and bond funds ourselves.

In this vein, the portfolio I recommend contains only two ETFs:

1. For the equity portion: the Vanguard Total World Stock Index Fund ETF (VT), which includes stocks of more than 9,000 American and international companies.

2. For the bond portion: the Vanguard Short-Term Bond ETF (BSV), which contains U.S. government, high-quality corporate, and investment-grade international dollar-denominated bonds.

Once we determine the proportion of stocks and bonds we want in our portfolio (as discussed in Chapter 4), we simply buy these two funds (VT and BSV), then go take a nap, watch Netflix, or toast a bagel. In short, that's it.

From 2013 to 2023, this diversified portfolio had annualized returns ranging from 5% (for a 60% stocks and 40% bonds portfolio) to 6.3% (for a more aggressive 80% stocks/20% bonds portfolio). This means that $10,000 invested hypothetically 10 years ago is worth between $16,300 and $18,400 today. And the expense ratios for these two funds are incredibly small: they represent an annual 0.07% and 0.04% of the portfolio size respectively.

You'll notice the stocks ETF I suggest contains U.S. as well as international stocks. Investors often ask if they could just invest in the U.S. stock market instead. It's far from a crazy idea since the U.S. market already has international exposure: on average, S&P 500 companies get around 30% of their revenue from outside the U.S.[90] I personally like the diversification international stocks provide. Also, U.S. stocks have outperformed international stocks over the last decade and a half, but there's no guarantee that this will continue to be the case in the future, or even that this trend couldn't reverse.

In any case, one of the best ways to invest only in U.S. stocks for people who want to do so is simply to buy the Vanguard S&P 500 ETF (VOO), which has an annual fee of 0.03%.

Also, these funds all pay a dividend to the shareholders who own them. These dividends are usually paid out in cash four times a year and can be automatically reinvested (free of charge) by most brokerage platforms in the purchase of new fund shares. When we open our account, we are asked to specify whether we want the dividends to be automatically reinvested, but we can do so at any time by contacting our brokerage firm.

Canadian investors can buy the diversified Vanguard All-Equity ETF Portfolio (VEQT) for the stock portion of their assets, and the CI 1-5 Year Laddered Government Strip Bond Index ETF (BXF) for the bonds portion.

Investors in the U.K. can buy the Vanguard S&P 500 ETF (VUSA) for exposure to U.S. stocks, and the The iShares Core FTSE 100 (ISF) for exposure to the U.K. stock market. For the bonds portion, iShares Global Govt Bond UCITS ETF (IGLH) is diversified and can be easily bought and sold on the London Stock Exchange.

Multi-asset ETFs

The portfolio I just recommended contains two funds. It's not much, but it's still more than one.

To further simplify your portfolio, you can choose a single multi-asset ETF. These funds are already diversified and balanced, including U.S. and international stocks as well as bonds.

By purchasing just one fund, an investor can therefore acquire the shares of thousands of companies around the world as well as thousands of bonds issued by Western governments.

This is the option I have chosen for my smaller accounts, such as my Roth IRA. I don't want any hassle or extra work with these accounts, and buying a single ETF and contributing to it every year works well for me. I like the minimalist look of these funds: clicking on my account and seeing only a single line of text and numbers makes me feel like I've done my homework, or have a tidy kitchen. Something like that.

In this category, the iShares Core Growth Allocation ETF (AOR) is composed of 80% stocks traded in the U.S. and several other countries, and 20% bonds issued by the U.S. government and other developed countries. The iShares Core Moderate Allocation ETF (AOM) is a more conservative version of this fund. It consists of 50% U.S. and international stocks, and 50% U.S. government bonds. The expense ratio of these funds is 0.15%.

For Canadian investors, an equivalent fund would be Vanguard's Growth ETF Portfolio (VGRO), with an expense ratio of 0.24%.

Another avenue available to U.S. investors who want to save for retirement is to buy a target-date fund. These funds assume that you will retire in a certain year, say 2040, or 2050, so the asset mix in the fund changes over time to reflect the need for more stability as this date approaches. For example, one can buy the VTIVX Vanguard Target Retirement 2045 Index Fund directly from Vanguard USA (this would be if you plan to retire in 2045). There is a $1,000 investment minimum, and the management fees are 0.08%.

Investors in the United Kingdom can look for the Vanguard LifeStrategy family of index funds, which are offered in different versions, from 20% in stocks to 100% in stocks, and have a management fee of 0.27%.

Studies have shown that investors who buy all-in-one funds tend to behave better and end up with more money than investors who buy multiple funds, because all-in-one funds make it harder to try to speculate or time the market.

CHOOSING ESG INVESTING

When we buy an ETF, we become a co-owner of thousands of companies. We may not agree with the actions of some of these companies – for example, they may produce fossil fuels, weapons, or tobacco products. Buying the "whole market" in this way can be contrary to our values.

To address this, some ETFs exclude certain companies based on environmental, social and governance criteria, an investment choice known as ESG.

ESG funds may exclude different types of industries, including alcohol, civilian firearms, controversial weapons, conventional weapons, private prisons, gambling, etc. They however sometimes keep the "least bad" of the companies in an industry, so I encourage you to read the details of the funds you are interested in.

ETFs that meet ESG criteria are increasingly in demand, with projections showing that they will account for the majority of new investments over the next few years. This trend has begun to push companies to do better on the environmental front to avoid being excluded from these new financial products.

To give an example, BlackRock, iShares MSCI USA ESG Enhanced UCITS ETF (EDMU) offers exposure to a portfolio of U.S. stocks from companies that have pledged to exceed decarbonization for an EU Climate Transition Benchmark. The management fee for this fund is a very reasonable 0.07% per year.

In Canada, an equivalent ETF would be the iShares ESG Aware MSCI Canada Index ETF (XESG), with an expense ratio of 0.16%.

U.K.-based investors can invest in the iShares MSCI UK IMI ESG Leaders UCITS ETF (UKEL), which offers broad exposure to U.K. companies with "high environmental, social, and governance performance relative to their sector peers," and has an expense ratio of 0.15%.

If your ETFs are not ESG, all is not lost. That's because, contrary to popular belief, with the exception of a brand-new stock launch, buying a company's stock does not fund that company. For example, the $1,000 we pay for Apple stock does not end up in Apple's pocket, but in the pocket of the person or institution that held the stock before selling it to us. We can debate the ethical issue of owning part of a company we disagree with. But our money does not help that company fund its operations. If the market doesn't need it anymore, like the market didn't need Sears or Kodak, for example, that company will see its value melt away and it may eventually be delisted or declare bankruptcy.

Asking for help

Buying an ETF in a brokerage account is simple, but there are a few details to know. For example, at the time of purchase, you may have to calculate the number of units of the fund you can buy with the amount you want to invest. Also, the interface offers us two prices for the fund: the "bid price" and the "ask price," which usually vary by a few cents. The principle is the same as buying or selling currencies in a currency exchange booth at an international airport: when buying, we must look at the highest price (the "ask price"), and when selling, we must consider the one that is slightly lower (the "bid price"). It is by pocketing this difference of a few cents that the firm that handles the transaction makes a profit.

If you're just starting to invest on your own and are intimidated by the process of opening a brokerage account or buying an ETF, I suggest a not-so-high-tech but effective solution: call the customer service department of the institution where you have your brokerage account. Employees can answer your questions and help you take your first steps as an investor.

Should you rebalance your portfolio?

Rebalancing your index ETF portfolio means sitting down once a year or so to buy or sell a small portion of your assets to restore the proportion of stocks and bonds we originally chose. For example, a 60% stocks and 40% bonds portfolio will be out of balance after a year in which stocks have risen strongly. We may see, for example, that the value of our portfolio is now weighted at 66% in stocks and 34% bonds.

We can then sell some of the stocks ETF and buy some of the bond ETF as required to return to the 60/40 allocation.

The advantage of this method is that it encourages us to sell stocks when they have risen in value, and to buy them when they have fallen. This is a psychologically difficult thing for investors to do, so the rebalancing provides a helpful process for us to follow to carry out this task. However, the main objective of rebalancing is not to maximize returns, but to minimize risk. Without rebalancing, the stocks portion of our portfolio will probably sooner or later outpace the bonds portion, which could be a concern in the event of a sudden market decline. Another way to rebalance is simply to buy more of the laggard fund when adding fresh money to our portfolio.

John Bogle, the founder of Vanguard, was not a big advocate of portfolio rebalancing, and chose not to do it himself for his own investments. Bogle calculated that over all 25-year periods since 1826, a portfolio composed of 50% U.S. stocks and 50% bonds ended up worth more 52% of the time when rebalanced each year. "In my opinion, this small difference is statistically meaningless," he wrote.

His conclusion: each investor is free to decide whether to rebalance their portfolio. "Rebalancing is a personal choice, not a choice that statistics can validate. There's certainly nothing the matter with doing it (although I don't do it myself), but also no reason to slavishly worry about small changes in the equity ratio. Maybe, for example, if your 50% equity position grew to, say, 55% or 60%... [...] Use your own judgment."[91]

Advantages and disadvantages of discount brokerage

Advantages

- Lowest expense ratio on the market.
- Full access to stock and bond ETFs or index funds.
- Perfect for long-term investing.

Disadvantages

- No barriers to bad behavior (e.g., selling in a correction, not investing enough money, etc.).
- Requires some learning to make transactions.
- No professional advice.
- We must trade when the market is open (Monday to Friday, 9:30 a.m. to 4:00 p.m., except holidays).

2. ROBO-ADVISORS

Investors who are uncomfortable with the idea of investing through a brokerage account can use robo-advisors.

These automated digital platforms make ETFs accessible to anyone with a smartphone.

Some of the big names in these platforms include Vanguard Personal and Digital Advisor Services, Schwab Intelligent Portfolios, Betterment, and Wealthfront.

These services are primarily aimed at younger investors, but investors of all ages can benefit. Once set up, our investments run on autopilot, and we don't have to pay attention to them.

The main advantage of these services is their simplicity: they take a daunting task (investing) and turn it into something familiar and simple to perform (as simple as transferring money from one account to another).

When we open an account, on our computer or phone, these platforms ask us to answer a few questions about our goals and our tolerance for the risk of seeing the value of our investments fall.

Based on our responses, the platform assembles a diversified portfolio consisting of a series of index ETFs representing U.S., international and emerging markets, as well as bonds.

Then we deposit money into our investment account, and we're done. We don't have to buy funds and sell them, or even rebalance our portfolio back to the original allocation between stock and bond ETFs. It's all done for us. We can also withdraw our money at any time.

Like the brokerage arm of the banking institutions, these platforms allow us to open an IRA, Roth IRA, and other types of accounts.

Also, their graphical interface shows us what our investments could be worth in 10, 20, or 30 years. This can be a reassuring element in a market storm. Does the investor who has $35,000 in investments really want to sell it all and give up having, for example, $70,000 in 10 years, $140,000 in 20 years, or $280,000 in 30 years? The platform won't prevent investors from pulling out money during a stock market crash, but at least it can make them think twice before they sell.

Most robo-advisors make money by charging fees that represent a small portion of the portfolio's value – usually less than 1%. Others, like Schwab Intelligent Portfolios, charge no fees but require a minimum of $5,000 in the account.

However, the strength of robo-advisors (removing humans from the activity of investing) is also their Achilles heel: when we invest our money, we like to be able to talk to someone. These platforms have understood this and now offer their clients the opportunity to call, email or schedule a video chat with a human advisor who can help them optimize their portfolio.

For an even more personalized one-on-one meeting, investors can also hire an outside independent financial planner on a fee-for-service basis who can analyze their finances from start to finish, write a detailed report, and answer their specific tax or retirement questions.

For example, the financial planner will be able to suggest an asset allocation between stocks and bonds that suits the client's age, income, and future needs.

The client can then set up this allocation in their robo-advisor or in their discount brokerage accounts.

Having a financial life analysis done by an independent financial planner can cost a few thousand dollars, a bill that increases if several types of assets are involved, such as real estate investments.

Advantages and disadvantages of automated management platforms

Advantages

- Lower than average expense ratio.

- Diversified ETF portfolios at the click of a button.

- Simple and intuitive interface.

- Advice from professionals.

Disadvantages

- Medium barrier to bad behavior (e.g., selling in a correction).

- Potentially limited access to human advisors.

---

3. DOING BUSINESS
WITH A PROFESSIONAL

The third option is the most expensive in terms of fees, but the simplest and most reassuring for everything else: deal with a professional.

Let's face it: managing large sums of money is not for everyone, and it can be appealing to have a professional take care of our investments for us. I completely understand that, and having read this book so far, if you choose to work with a professional then you will do so with full knowledge of the facts.

We're talking about a greater investment of time per year – if only to take an interest in our investments or meet with the professional who looks after our assets. This investment of time is not a handicap here: we want to know what's going on with our investments – and have the peace of mind of knowing that someone knowledgeable about the markets has their hands on the wheel.

The following is a non-exhaustive list of the types of companies and professionals that can help us manage our investments.

Investment advisor

An investment advisor (sometimes spelled adviser, with an "e") is an individual or company who is paid for providing the client with advice and managing their investments.

According to the Financial Industry Regulatory Authority (FINRA), common names for investment advisors include asset managers, investment counselors, investment managers, portfolio managers, and wealth managers (catering to high-net-worth individuals). Investment advisors working for registered investment advisor firms (RIAs) have a fiduciary duty to their clients: they must recommend the best products for their needs, not the product that pays them the highest fees. Investment advisers who manage $110 million or more in client assets must register with the Securities and Exchange Commission (SEC).

In this field, the gold standard is the Chartered Financial Analyst (CFA) designation, which is hard to obtain and ensures that the person managing our investments is competent and knowledgeable.

In 2019, investment advisors working for RIAs charged a total advisory fee of 1.17% of assets under management per year.[92] Some investment advisors work on a fee-only basis and typically charge a few thousand dollars to create a financial plan, which can be cheaper than paying recurring annual fees on the value of our portfolio. The National Association of Personal Financial Advisors (NAPFA) website is a good place to search for a fee-only investment advisor.

Financial planner

Financial planners offer advice on finances, taxation, retirement, estate, investments, insurance, and other areas.

They can develop a plan of action adapted to our needs, constraints, and objectives. They may also sell investments, insurance, or other financial products.

The financial planning profession does not have its own regulator. Some planners might hold a credential such as the Certified Financial Planner designation, or CFP, issued by the Certified Financial Planner Board of Standards. "This designation requires at least three years of experience, imposes fairly rigorous standards to earn and maintain, allows investors to verify the status of anyone claiming to be a CFP and has a disciplinary process," says FINRA.[93]

Some financial planners work on a fee-only basis and do not collect commissions on the products they recommend.

Accountant

According to FINRA, accountants are trained to provide "professional assistance to individuals and companies in areas including tax and financial planning, tax reporting, auditing, and management consulting." Accountants should have the Certified Public Accountant (CPA) credential. Some accountants may sell investments, but their main professional focus is the U.S. tax code.

Family office

Families drowning in money might want help with financial planning, insurance, charitable giving, estate planning, tax planning, etc. This is where a family office comes in. A single-family office can serve just one ultra-affluent family, while multi-family offices (MFOs) can serve many. MFOs typically get paid by taking a percentage of the assets under management: according to one study, the average minimum annual fee in the U.S. is $92,897 per year.[94]

———

Whether we are dealing with an investment advisor, a wealth manager, or a financial planner, I recommend that we test our investment professional before we start or continue to do business with them.

Let's inform them that our investment preference is a diversified portfolio of index ETFs with a very low expense ratio. If the response we receive is anything other than "Great!" or "I already did!" then we should continue our search.

Chances are that some professionals will recommend that we invest in mutual funds – which historically have been the bread and butter of this industry. Let's ask them questions and discuss the concepts explained in this book. Let's also ask them to give us the sources to back up what they're saying – and, no, the promotional material produced by the company that pays their salary doesn't count.

Advantages and disadvantages of dealing with a professional

Advantages

- One person takes care of our investments.
- Personalized service.
- Tax optimization.
- High barrier to bad behavior (e.g., selling in a correction).
- Can encourage us to save and invest more.

Disadvantages

- Potentially high fees.
- Potentially restricted access to index ETFs.
- Our interests may conflict with those of the financial institution.

No matter which investment method we choose, the important thing is to take the first step and not to complicate things.

When asked about the type of training that has allowed her to win so many races in her career, U.S. marathon champion and Olympic gold medalist Joan Benoit said that she leaves her house, goes to the end of her driveway, and she either turns left or turn right. "My philosophy on running is this: I don't dwell on it, I do it." And there you have it.

CONCLUSION:
THE COW AND
THE SHARK

Going to the moon is not that far. The longest journey
is the journey inward.

Anaïs Nin, author

D URING A FAMILY vacation on Cape Cod a few years
ago we spotted a white shark.

Lifeguards have developed an effective system to protect
people from sharks. They are stationed at regular intervals
along miles of beaches, and they scan the horizon with
binoculars. If a lifeguard sees a shark, they communicate
by radio with their colleagues. Whistles are blown all along
the coast, no-swimming flags are hoisted on top of poles,

and thousands of swimmers must get out of the water for an hour.

During one of these no-swimming episodes, we saw a group of vacationers running to the ocean. Curious, we did the same. In front of us, about 50 feet away, a gray fin split the waves, causing terrified screams on the beach – just like in the movies.

Although they are large and frightening, sharks do not rank high on the list of the most dangerous animals for humans.

Did you know that sharks kill fewer people than cows?

Sharks cause an average of five deaths per year worldwide, while cows cause an average of 22 recorded deaths, including by kicking or trampling their victims.

Cows kill four times more humans than sharks.

Sharks are terrifying, and each of their attacks makes headlines around the globe. Cows are anything but terrifying.

The paradox of the cow and the shark sums up the world of investing.

We don't fear the right things in investing. We are afraid of the shark (market crash, a missed opportunity, the next recession, etc.), while much less spectacular risks can hurt us much more (buying stocks that are supposed to make us rich, waiting before starting to invest, selling in anticipation of a stock market crash, paying a high expense ratio, etc.).

The "shark" type risks are very visible. When they appear, every fiber of our being pays attention to them.

The "cow" risks are invisible. They are rarely mentioned. They should challenge us, but they have nothing to impress us. So they are simply ignored.

I also like the cow and shark analogy because the image of the shark is often associated with the world of finance. The shark is the ambitious professional who would not hesitate to sell his mother a questionable investment if he could make a profit.

But, as this book has shown, almost all sharks have worse returns than cows, which just graze on the grass and watch the trains go by without worrying about the growth of their balanced investments.

When it comes to risk, we all have a hard time telling the difference. What looks threatening is not always threatening. And real threats are often difficult to distinguish.

For example, while everyone fears a dramatic scenario such as a stock market crash, another more mundane scenario can hurt us much more: not investing enough. The investor who is obsessed with the daily rise and fall of his $30,000 investments portfolio may not realize that adding $6,000 to his investments automatically increases them by 20%.

When we're in our first few years of investing, the biggest danger is not that our assets will go down. The greatest danger is not investing enough. To expect the markets to do the work for us, and then to panic if they don't.

Our brain is not made to invest. It is conditioned to avoid uncertainty and seek security. When it sees the value of our investments rise, it floats in a bath of endorphins and imagines a bright future, until a sudden drop occurs, dragging along its eternal companions, fear and doubt.

EVERYBODY MAKES MISTAKES

I'm fascinated by a now-forgotten moment in the history of Larry Page and Sergey Brin, the co-founders of Google. In 1999, when Google had only a half-dozen employees working at beige computers in a Silicon Valley garage, Page and Brin wanted to sell their company. Through an intermediary they told the head of Excite, the internet portal that dominated the market at the time, that they were willing to accept a million dollars for Google.

Their offer was rejected.

Then they indicated that they were willing to accept $750,000.

Their offer was rejected again.

Today, Page and Brin are among the 10 richest people in the world, with a combined net worth of nearly $200 billion.

No investor has a crystal ball. Not you. Nor me. Nor the boss of Excite. Nor the co-founders of Google.

I noted earlier in this book that many investment professionals discourage their clients from investing without their help. I agree with this recommendation, but not for the same reason they do.

> I want to accumulate assets, not responsibilities.
>
> *James Clear, author and investor*

I think most people should not be self-directed investors because they don't have an interest in it. They're not comfortable managing large amounts of money, they're afraid of making a mistake, picking the wrong fund, not confident in their ability, etc.

I don't condemn that, I think it's perfectly normal. But I also believe that many people can manage their own investments. If you have read this book so far, I congratulate you, because you are certainly part of this group.

The ability of people to adapt their behavior to particular situations is often underestimated. During the COVID-19 crisis, for example, the media reported relentlessly on stories of people gathering despite public health guidelines, celebrating without masks, and protesting against these "freedoms" being taken away.

What the media did not show were the billions of people around the world who changed their behavior in rapid and unprecedented ways to slow the spread of the virus. The millions of businesses and companies that switched to telecommuting overnight to protect their employees and customers.

Wearing a mask in public, which was previously almost never seen outside of Asia, became commonplace from Chicago to Sydney.

Humans learn. Humans adapt. It's even what we know how to do best!

EXPONENTIAL AND PASSIVE

I have a hard time explaining to myself why I am interested in the investment world.

I did not study in this field, my parents and family were not interested in it. I have a limited attention span for economic news. I don't know the U.S. Fed Funds Rate by heart. I am also not attracted to luxurious objects, beautiful cars, expensive vacations, or fancy clothes.

So why am I interested in money and the best practices to make it grow?

I am attracted to the combination of two extremes: the passive and the exponential aspect of investing.

I work and earn a salary. Once invested, my salary also starts working, and earning money. After 15 or 20 years, my investments earn almost as much per year as I do.

And it floors me.

I also like the sense of detachment that investing imposes when practiced well. The Roman philosopher Seneca wrote over 2,000 years ago that we should aspire to control our reaction to negative events in life just like the lion tamer puts his hand in the animal's mouth, or the guard gives the tiger a kiss.

"Similarly, the wise person is a skilled expert at taming misfortune. Pain, poverty, disgrace, imprisonment, and exile are feared by everyone. But when they encounter the wise person, they are tamed."

Posted on the wall of my office, this quote has accompanied me during stock market crashes. If the crashes experienced several years ago scared me, the most recent ones left me indifferent.

Just like the tiger that opens its mouth and roars, the numbers in red on the screen do everything to try to scare us, to make us react. Our job is to say, "Thanks, but it's not working. Nice try, sorry."

Finally, I like the fact that stock market investing doesn't care about who we are personally, i.e., it doesn't care about our ego, our degrees, our salary, where we were born, the size of our house, or the make of our car.

In the eyes of the market, none of this matters. In investing, a high school dropout can be more successful than a business school-educated executive will ever be. The idea that such a thing is not only possible, but commonplace, will never cease to fascinate me.

NO SELF-PITY

In these pages, I've mentioned Charlie Munger, Warren Buffett's billionaire right-hand man, several times. At 99 years of age, Charlie Munger is one of the great investors of our time. It's a pleasure to read and listen to his speeches. He's extremely erudite – the man is a veritable quote machine. But his life has been very difficult.

In 1953, as a 29-year-old lawyer, Charlie Munger divorced his first wife. The couple had three young children. The separation was devastating: Charlie lost almost everything, including his home. He was living in a university dormitory and driving a car that was in such bad shape that even his children pointed it out to him.

A year later, his son Teddy was diagnosed with leukemia, the blood cancer that was incurable at the time. Teddy had to be transferred to a hospital in Pasadena, California, to a children's hospice unit, "one of the saddest places on earth," Charlie once said.

Charlie and his ex-wife would go to the hospital to visit their bedridden son, who was getting weaker every day. A friend said Charlie would go into the hospital, hold his young son, and then walk the streets of Pasadena crying.

Teddy Munger died the following year at the age of nine.

At 31, Charlie was divorced, had just buried his son, was broke, and had a large hospital bill to pay.

In a fascinating essay on Munger's life, author Safal Niveshak writes, "It would have been tempting for him to just give it all up and turn to vices (alcohol, drugs) as so many around him had done at that time. But Charlie was not that man and he kept going."[95]

A few years later, in 1959, Charlie met Warren Buffett at a dinner party. The two men knew right away that they were meant to work together.

Warren and Charlie built the Berkshire Hathaway conglomerate, now one of the largest companies in the world, with over 350,000 employees and annual revenues of more than $275 billion. Charlie remarried and had four more children with his new wife.

Bad luck did not leave him. In his fifties, he became blind in his left eye after an operation for cataracts that went wrong. This event was difficult to accept for a man who considers reading his favorite activity – the duty of anyone who wants to learn and improve. His eye hurt so much that it had to be replaced with a glass eye.

In a speech to graduating law students at the University of Southern California (USC) a few years ago, Charlie Munger said that one of the lessons he learned from the misfortunes in his life was to never feel sorry for himself.

"Generally speaking, envy, resentment, revenge, and self-pity are disastrous modes of thought," he said. "Every time you find you're drifting into self-pity, I don't care what the cause, your child could be dying from cancer, self-pity is not going to improve the situation. It's a ridiculous way to behave. Life will have terrible blows, horrible blows, unfair blows, it doesn't matter. Some people recover and others don't. [...] Every mischance in life [is] an opportunity to learn something and that your duty [is] not to be immersed in self-pity, but to utilize the terrible blow in a constructive fashion." [96]

The important thing, says Charlie, is to always get back up. No life is perfect.

This lesson is applicable to all aspects of our lives, and it is also applicable in investment.

We can have failures in investing. The important thing is to learn, keep our head up and keep moving forward. "I don't like any feeling of being victimized," Munger once said. "I'm not a victim. I'm a survivor."

VALID SOLUTION

I placed a quote from Arthur Conan Doyle, the author of *The Adventures of Sherlock Holmes*, at the beginning of this book. I wanted to suggest that you, the reader, try to put yourself in the shoes of the famous detective.

How would Sherlock Holmes approach the investment world?

Once all the facts are in and his few oblique questions are answered, I imagine the famous detective walking past the high-fee mutual fund salesmen and deciding to put his pounds into a portfolio of index ETFs, before forgetting about them and moving on to his next investigation.

As you read through this book, some may say that I've made up my mind. That I am ignoring other valid methods of stock market investing to give full play to ETF investing. I will answer that I have never been guided by any philosophy or investment method that I would have fallen in love with: I base myself on facts. As I explain in the Preface, I did not start my quest with the answers presented in this book in mind. I have accumulated this information and these principles year after year, often at the cost of humiliating mistakes.

This book does not attempt to tell you what to do, but rather to present a method of investing that has been independently studied, rigorously researched, and has produced results that are more impressive and reliable than virtually any other way to approach the markets.

I know that for some, the advice to "buy ETFs and move on" is not a valid solution. It's not satisfying; it's not a philosophy that reflects who they are and what they want to accomplish in life.

If this is your case, I'm not saying that you shouldn't be an active investor, that you shouldn't do stock picking. I want you to know that outperforming the market indexes (even by 1% or 2% annually) is an exceptional achievement, often impossible to sustain for more than a few years, and that examples of underperformance are as numerous as success stories are rare.

A LITTLE REMOVED
FROM THE WORLD

Since I was a kid, I like to calculate how long I can stay underwater in a lake while holding my breath.

I like that feeling of calm, of control. Knowing that with each attempt, I get a little better. Realizing that my body is working to keep me alive as three feet of water separate me from the open air as I enter my third minute without breathing.

Underwater, I am removed from the world and I am part of it at the same time.

Investing is a similar experience. We must learn to be calm, to stir as little as possible in an environment that has everything to make us react. We must refuse to let our emotions control us. We must realize that everything is better when we are a little removed from the world.

Above all, we must take pleasure in postponing the moment when we come to the surface, slowly, calmly, to take a breath of air, as on the first day, before diving back into the silence.

NOTES

1   Michael Lewis, *The Big Short: Inside the Doomsday Machine*, W. W. Norton & Company, 2010.

2   Gregory Zuckerman, *The Greatest Trade Ever: The Behind-the-scenes Story of How John Paulson Defied Wall Street and Made Financial History*, Crown Business, 2009.

3   Rupert Hargreaves, "Warren Buffett: Learn From Your Mistakes and Move Forward," Yahoo Finance, October 16, 2018.

4   Steven Novella, "Lessons from Dunning-Kruger," NeuroLogica blog, November 6, 2014.

5   Andrew Odlyzko, "Newton's financial misadventures in the South Sea Bubble," *Notes and Records*, August 29, 2018.

6   Ibid.

7   Independent publication, 2021.

8   Andrew Edgecliffe-Johnson, "Lunch with the FT: Henry Blodget," *Financial Times*, November 15, 2013.

9   William Green, *Richer, Wiser, Happier: How the World's Greatest Investors Win in Markets and Life*, Scribner, 2021, p. 3.

10 Burton Malkiel, *A Random Walk Down Wall Street: The Time-Tested Strategy for Successful Investing*, W. W. Norton, 2009, p. 264.

11 Warren Buffett, Berkshire Hathaway shareholder letter, 2008, p. 16.

12 SPIVA website, consulted by the author on October 13, 2022.

13 "Missing Out: Millennials and the Markets," Ontario Securities Commission, November 27, 2017.

14 "Our results," Caisse de dépôt et placement du Québec website, 2021.

15 "Harvard's billion-dollar farmland fiasco," GRAIN report, September 6, 2018.

16 Tim Edwards et al, "SPIVA Institutional Scorecard Year-End 2021," S&P Global, September 8, 2022.

17 Gregory Zuckerman, "This Is Unbelievable: A Hedge Fund Star Dims, and Investors Flee," *The Wall Street Journal*, July 1, 2018.

18 Burton Malkiel, *Random Walk*, p. 167.

19 David R. Harper, "Hedge Funds: Higher Returns or Just High Fees?" Investopedia, April 12, 2021.

20 Raymond Kerzérho, "The Terrible Truth about Hedge Funds," PWLCapital, August 23, 2021.

21 Warren Buffett, Berkshire Hathaway shareholder letter, 2016, p. 24.

22 Hendrik Bessembinder, "Do Stocks Outperform Treasury Bills?" Arizona State University, August 22, 2017.

23 Thomas Macpherson, "Bessembinder Rocks the Investment World," GuruFocus, October 19, 2017.

24 Ben Carlson and Michael Batnick, "A Random Talk with Burton Malkiel," Animal Spirits podcast, October 2, 2020.

25 Ibid.

26 Stephen J. Dubner, "The Stupidest Thing You Can Do With Your Money," Freakonomics podcast, September 21, 2017.

27 John C. Bogle, *The Little Book of Common Sense Investing: The Only Way to Guarantee Your Fair Share of Stock Market Returns*, Wiley, 2017, p. 184.

28 Warren Buffett, op. cit., p. 24.

29 Ben Carlson and Michael Batnick, op. cit.

30 Stephen A. Jarislowsky, *Dans la jungle du placement*, Les Éditions Transcontinental, 2005, p. 27.

31 Tim Edwards et al, "The Volatility of Active Management," S&P Global, August 2016.

32 Emmie Martin, "Warren Buffett wants 90 percent of his wealth to go to this one investment after he's gone," CNBC, February 27, 2019.

33 Charles V. Harlow and Michael D. Kinsman, "The Electric Day Trader and Ruin," *Pepperdine Graziadio Business Review*, 1999.

34 Brad M. Barber et al, "Trading Is Hazardous to Your Wealth: The Common Stock Investment Performance

of Individual Investors," *The Journal of Finance*, April 2000.

35 William Bernstein, *The Four Pillars of Investing: Lessons for Building a Winning Portfolio*, McGraw-Hill, Kindle version, 2010, p. 216.

36 John Bogle, *The Little Book of Common Sense Investing*, Wiley, 2017, Kindle format.

37 Ibid., p. 168.

38 Roger Collier, "The challenges of physician retirement," *Canadian Medical Association Journal*, January 16, 2017.

39 Ibid.

40 Daniel Solin, "Why Smart Doctors and Dentists Make Dumb Investors," AOL, December 23, 2009.

41 Jonathan Satovsky, "Smart People Can Make Stupid Investing Decisions," *Forbes*, August 16, 2012.

42 Oliver Sung, "Charlie Munger: 2021 Daily Journal Annual Meeting Transcript," Junto Investments, February 26, 2021.

43 Jason Zweig, "False profits," Jasonzweig.com, June 23, 2015.

44 David Zuckerman, "Initial Public Offerings Historical Returns," Financial Planning Association, January 31, 2012.

45 Ibid.

46 Alessio Emanuele Biondo et al, "Are Random Trading Strategies More Successful than Technical Ones?" *PLoS ONE*, July 11, 2013.

47 Retirement 101, "Returning to the Original Strategy," July 15, 2020.

48 Ibid.

49 Andrew Hallam, *Millionaire Teacher: The Nine Rules of Wealth You Should Have Learned in School*, Wiley, 2017.

50 Andrew Hallam, "Do I Regret Selling Stocks Worth $700,000?" Andrewhallam.com, September 2, 2011.

51 Claire Boyte-White, "How Dividends Affect Stock Prices," Investopedia, July 26, 2020.

52 Simon Sinek, *The Infinite Game*, Penguin, 2019, p. 12.

53 Fox Butterfield, "From Ben Franklin, a Gift That's Worth Two Fights," *The New York Times*, April 21, 1990.

54 Stephan A. Schwartz, "Ben Franklin's Gift that Keeps on Giving," *American History*, February 2009.

55 Myles Udland, "Fidelity Reviewed Which Investors Did Best And What They Found Was Hilarious," Business Insider, September 4, 2014.

56 Jim O'Shaughnessy, "Jason Zweig – Psychology, History & Writing," Infinite Loops podcast, January 28, 2021.

57 "The Theft That Made The 'Mona Lisa' A Masterpiece," NPR, July 30, 2011.

58 Jennifer Booton, "Jim Cramer doesn't beat the market," MarketWatch, May 16, 2016.

59 Josh Brown, "Why I don't wake up to the news," thereformedbroker.com, June 4, 2019.

60 Ibid.

61 Benjamin Graham, *The Intelligent Investor: The Definitive Book on Value Investing*, Harper Business, p. 48.

62 "The 2018 forecast: rising risks to the status quo," Vanguard Canada, December 7, 2017.

63 Joe Chidley, "Gut feeling: U.S. rally will fizzle, Chinese stocks will surge and TSX will climb higher in 2017," *Financial Post*, December 29, 2016.

64 Guru Grades, CXO Advisory Group, https://www. cxoadvisory.com/gurus.

65 Larry Swedroe, "You Make More Money Selling Advice Than Following It," CBS News, May 20, 2010.

66 Craig Botham and Irene Lauro, "Climate change and financial markets," Schroders, February 2020.

67 Swiss Re Institute, "The economics of climate change: no action not an option," April 2021.

68 Christopher Flavelle, "Climate Change Could Cut World Economy by $23 Trillion in 2050, Insurance Giant Warns," *The New York Times*, April 22, 2021.

69 Nicolas Bérubé, "Un optimiste dans la grisaille," *La Presse Affaires*, February 19, 2013.

70 Ibid.

71 Walter Isaacson, *Benjamin Franklin: An American Life*, Simon & Schuster, 2003, p. 267.

72 Dana Anspach, "How to Handle Stock Market Corrections," *The Balance*, December 1, 2020.

73 Thomas Franck, "Here's how long stock market corrections last and how bad they can get," CNBC, February 27, 2020.

74 David Koenig, "Market Corrections Are More Common Than You Might Think," Charles Schwab Intelligent Portfolios, February 25, 2022.

75 Morgan Housel, *The Psychology of Money*, Harriman House, 2020, p. 160.

76 Ben Carlson, "All-Time Highs Are Both Scary & Normal," A Wealth of Common Sense, November 29, 2019.

77 Ben Carlson, "2018 vs. 2019 in the Stock Market," A Wealth of Common Sense, January 21, 2020.

78 Ben Carlson, "What Happens After the Stock Market is Up Big?" A Wealth of Common Sense, April 11, 2021.

79 Garth Turner, "Suck it up," Greaterfool, April 15, 2021.

80 William Green, *Richer, Wiser, Happier*, p. 75.

81 H. Nejat Seyhun, "Stock market extremes and portfolio performance," Towneley Capital Management, 1994.

82 Warren Buffett Investment Strategy, Plan For 2020, YouTube, December 4, 2019.

83 Nick Maggiulli, "Why Market Timing Can Be So Appealing," Of Dollars And Data, January 20, 2020.

84 Patrick O'Shaughnessy, "Trail Magic – Lessons from Two Years of the Podcast," Invest Like the Best podcast, September 18, 2018.

85 Ron Lieber, "Les femmes, meilleures que les hommes?" *La Presse*, October 30, 2021.

86 Nicholas Hyett, "Do women make better investors?" Hargreaves Lansdown, January 29, 2018.

87 Jason Zweig, "Just How Dumb Are Investors?" *The Wall Street Journal*, May 9, 2014.

88 John C. Bogle, "The Arithmetic of "All-In" Investment Expenses," *Financial Analysts Journal*, 2014.

89 Brett Arends, "The inventor of the '4% rule' just changed it," MarketWatch, October 22, 2020.

90 Phillip Brzenk, "The Impact of the Global Economy on the S&P 500," S&P Global, March 19, 2018.

91 Tim McAleenan, "John Bogle Doesn't Rebalance His Portfolio," The Conservative Income Investor, November 5, 2019.

92 "2019 RIA Industry Study: Total Average Fee is 1.17%," RIA in a box, July 23, 2019.

93 Financial Industry Regulatory Authority (FINRA) Website, consulted by the author on October 28, 2022.

94 Tom Burroughes, "Family Offices, Wealth Houses Should Re-Think Fee Structures – Study," February 9, 2021.

95 Safal Niveshak, "A Story of Courage and Hope from the Life of Charlie Munger," safalniveshak.com, August 5, 2019.

96 Ibid.

ACKNOWLEDGMENTS

I F THIS BOOK has turned out to be anything more than an expensive coaster, it is because of the help, insights, and work of a small group of people whom I would like to thank.

Thank you to my wife Pénélope Fortier for her patience, her support and her words of encouragement that accompanied me during the writing of this book.

Thank you to Craig Pearce, senior commissioning editor at Harriman House, for believing in this book and bringing it to the world.

Thank you to Richard Morin for helping me with this project, and to Stephen A. Jarislowsky, Josée Jeffrey, Marc-André Turcot, Ian Gascon for opening their doors to me and speaking so generously about their careers and their profession. Thank you to Peter Adeney, Van-Anh Hoang, Jean-Sébastien Pilotte, Andrew Hallam, Morgan Housel, and Mohnish Pabrai.

Thank you to Véronique Bérubé and Laurent McComber for reading early drafts of this book and helping me clarify my thinking – any errors or omissions in this work are my own.

Thank you to Jean-François Bouchard, President of Éditions La Presse, and Pierre Cayouette, Publishing Director of Éditions La Presse. Thanks to Colette Lens for her insight and helpful suggestions.

ABOUT THE
AUTHOR

NICOLAS BÉRUBÉ is an award-winning financial writer and reporter with *La Presse*, one of Canada's largest news organizations. He lived in Los Angeles, California, for seven years as the paper's first West Coast correspondent, has received a National Newspaper Award and was a finalist for the Michener Awards, one of the highest honors in Canadian journalism. Initially published in French, *De Zéro à Millionnaire* was an instant bestseller in Canada.